Heather "Ping" Eckes

Kristin Van Risseghem

Sara Otto!

Andrea Lind

Katie St. Clair

Tami Siebenaler

Thanks for a great trip Michelle Kaupang

THE TRIP WAS EXCELLENT. Chris Dill

Shanda Greiner

Thank-You Soo much. This has been a memorable trip Brandy Siiks

sorry about spelling.

Kari Hilton

It's been real!

Erik Fair

Mindy Miller

Thanks for everything!! Ann Guibreth

Pat Siebenaler

Keri Cuyler

Scott Tourjer

sucks

Tracey Peterson

Jason Munson

Cory

alex San

Gretchen Haas

Jason Bell

Chris Doffing

Tara Dillon

Jason Reuter

Thanks for the great trip! Joy Lessard

Jeremy Witt

Thanks a Bunch!!

thanks! what a GREAT time a Great bunch of characters

Annette Raimann

Thanks for a great trip, Stephanie Mortholer

Mary Gilsett

Chance Munger

Tammi Riley

Thanks for all the hard work!! Suzie Bednarm

Kristine

Kansas City

A Celebration of the Heartland

Kansas City

A Celebration of the Heartland

Published by Hallmark Cards, Inc.

Book design by Vivian L. Strand

Printed in the United States of America
The Lowell Press, Kansas City, Missouri

ISBN 0-87529-631-9

This is dedicated to all those
who appreciate Kansas City
for what it is — and what it can be.

Contents

(left) The Scout in Penn Valley Park off Broadway at 27th is one of the area's best-known figures and stands for many as a symbol of Kansas City. Cast for the 1915 Panama-Pacific Exposition in San Francisco, the sculpture found fans when it was shown here in a national tour after the Exposition closed. Local citizens raised money to purchase the piece, which was installed in Penn Valley Park in 1922.

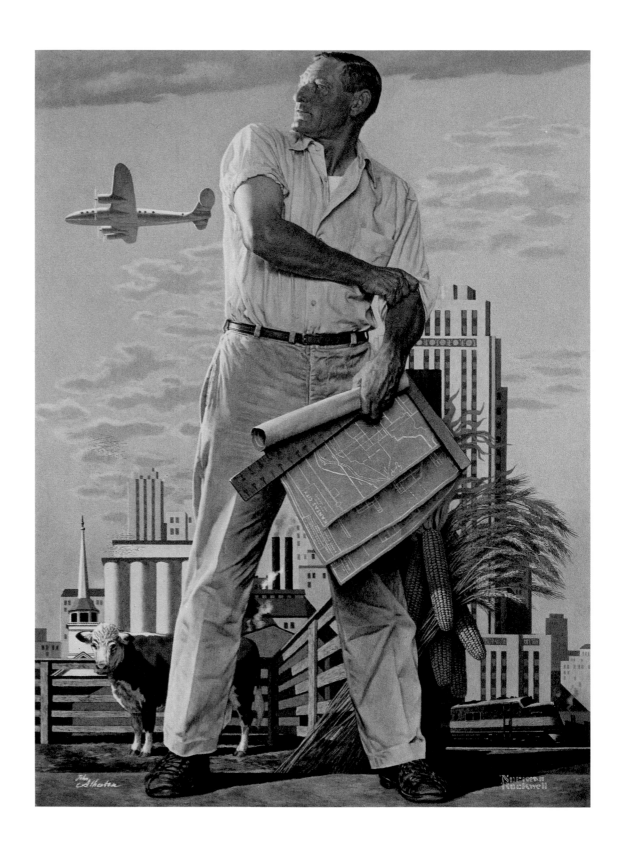

Foreword

The story of Kansas City is one of pioneers.

Not the larger-than-life figures of legend, although many have left their mark here.

Our pioneers more often have been ordinary people who possessed a vision of a better life, then set out to create it. People who were unafraid to labor at making a dream real or to stop and help neighbors build theirs as well.

One of the best expressions of this part of our history and temperament is found in Norman Rockwell's *Kansas City Spirit*. The painting was his contribution to rebuilding efforts after our devastating 1951 flood. It symbolized the vitality of those who build for the future, and the good in people that makes them put service above self.

By today's standards, the painting may seem quaint, its style old-fashioned. But not so the values it depicts: cooperation, gritty determination, hope for the future, confidence in knowing the worth of what is — and the value of what can be. *Kansas City Spirit* celebrates these timeless qualities.

To be sure, some aspects of the *Kansas City Spirit* would look different if it were painted today. Drawn to the fore would be a sense of strength and achievement that comes from our social, economic, political and cultural diversity. A new perspective would be added by the daily efforts of people who work, without thought of recognition, to constantly improve their part of the city. But it would still be framed by the stamina and resolve to build the kind of life in this area that gives us pride and enjoyment.

We hope this new edition of *Kansas City* is such a contemporary portrait of greater Kansas City. Its words and pictures are meant to document what has been created, and continues to be created today, from the *Kansas City Spirit*. And it is in that spirit that we offer it to the people who live here, their friends and our visitors.

Donald J. Hall
Chairman
Hallmark Cards, Inc.

Identity

The herders and the traders
and the sod corn crew;
They planted 'em a city when
the world was new;
They planted Kansas City
and the darn thing grew!

C. L. Edson
Kansas City poet
"Kansas City" (1920)

Many Faces, Many Dreams

Artists and photographers love the local light that makes even the ordinary seem splendid.

(opening) From a rude settlement on a rocky ledge, Kansas City has grown in only 150 years into a marvelous metropolis. The contemporary skyline signals a city ready for the future. The two rivers at its feet are a reminder of a fabled past.

(right) Score! The Kansas City Chiefs professional football team rolls on to victory. A winning team gives a collective boost to spectators and evaporates cultural, racial and ethnic differences by uniting residents in their enthusiasm for a cause.

I n the beginning, land drew the people here.

Undeniably, it was beautiful. Two broad rivers and uncounted streams ribboned a terrain broken by limestone bluffs, stretched by broad valleys and mantled with forests of hickory, oak and walnut. And over it all, a magical quality of wheaten-gold light suffused the land.

Beauty wasn't the real call, of course. It was wilderness. Frontier. Timber to cut. Fertile soil to plant. Grassy meadows to graze. It was the call of a spirit of place that silently promised *better* and *more.* The natural richness of the place beckoned, and people answered with many voices: *Home.*

Travelers by the tens of thousands arrived here planning to pass on through to the West. Many decided to stay. Some settled down gladly in the promising land. Others were just too tired or too broke to go on. So they stayed, too, and did what they knew best or what they could. But they all heard the silent promises the land offered.

Today the place generally called "Kansas City" is really a "regional city." It is 111 cities and towns in eight counties and two states and is one of the most ethnically diverse cities in the United States. Diversity characterizes not only the population but a great deal else as well.

Contrary to widely held and mistaken notions, Kansas City is not flat – either in geography or personality. It cannot be easily summarized for the same reason that jazz cannot be reduced to elevator music. Variations *are* the theme.

From the basics of climate to the niceties of style, Kansas City is unpredictable. There are,

for example, four distinct seasons, any two of which may be less than 12 hours apart. Autumn can bring swimming weather one day and snow the next. The man-made environment can be equally quixotic. Kansas City style cheerfully pairs *haute couture* suits and cowboy boots, big business with friendly farm. Cattle ruminate near the clustered high-tech companies of the "Silicon Prairie," separated from parking lots only by barbed wire and rows of the Osage orange bushes.

This community of contrasts is a surprising mix of ethnic, economic and cultural influences. Residents are used to travelers' amazement at the area's unexpected natural and designed beauty. Visitors are even more amazed by the enormous range of opportunities in business, education, the arts, recreation, services, shopping and residential neighborhoods.

Residents, on the other hand, are easily delighted but not overly surprised by much. They accept a great deal of variety as the norm. It's not that no standards exist. It's just that variety is part of the Kansas City *personality,* an unconscious blend of common sense and individual preference. Perhaps it is the legacy of frontier civility: friendly but not too nosy, helpful but independent, protective of everyone's right to be different.

Some of this personality came from the historical impossibility of homogenizing divergent groups of people. Lone newcomers might have blended in, but when the newcomers came in clusters — as they often did — they preserved their heritage even as they tried to adapt to a new life and a new community.

When they could, early immigrants came to this region in groups and tried to get jobs

The Missouri River flows through every chapter of the region's history. (above right) The Missouri Queen navigates the "Big Muddy," America's second-longest river after the Mississippi. At Kansas City, the Missouri is met by the Kansas River (above), which also is called the Kaw as a result of the way the Kanza Indians (now Kansa) pronounced their tribal name: Kauza. The rivers helped make Kansas City a center for commerce even before the coming of the railroads after the Civil War.

The "Muse of the Missouri" fountain between 8th and 9th on Main celebrates the river's importance in city life. Sculptor Wheeler Williams intended to model the fish in the Muse's net after native Missouri River fish but decided catfish were too ugly and carp had mouths too small to accommodate fountain jets. He created his own hybrid with a carp body and bluefish head.

together. Many Scandinavians went to work in the packing houses. Italians set up produce stalls at the City Market. Greeks worked as section-crews for the railroads. Bennelux farmers tilled the rich river bottoms.

Some incoming groups were larger than most frontier "cities." Five thousand Greek men arrived in Kansas City in one 14-year period and lived in rented rooms along Fifth Street in an area they called "Athens."

Three hundred Irish laborers were brought from Connaught County in 1856 by Father Bernard Donnelly to work a brick-yard in the Church's behalf, to cut roads through the bluffs and to help build the city's first Catholic cathedral. They settled near each other, as did the Irish immigrants that followed.

African-Americans brought to the area by white slaveholders made up a substantial percentage of the population prior to 1865. There were 4,000 slaves in Kansas City by 1860 (while the Irish, an increasingly domi-nant group in early Kansas City life, num-bered only 1,900 in 1865). Slaves were prohib-ited from gathering together except at church. As a result, their religious, social and political life became virtually inseparable.

This pattern of cohesion among people of like heritage or beliefs was repeated over the course of many decades with other foreign-born groups, including Italian Catholics, German Protestants and German Jews, Russian Mennonites, Russian Jews, Czechs, Serbs, Bohemians and Poles. They settled in enclaves, keeping alive the traditions they brought from their former homes.

Shared language, religious beliefs, cus-toms and tastes in food created neighbor-hoods in the growing Town of Kansas (as Kansas City, Missouri was then called) and in settlements along the Kansas and Missouri border. Descendants of some early settlers still preserve traditions in several areas of the metroplex today. Among the best known neighborhoods are Columbus Park, formerly called Little Italy, in the Northeast area of

Early Kansas City, Missouri earned the nickname "Gully Town" because its streets were gouged deeply through bluffs to the river banks. As late as the 1880s, when Kansas City's New York Life Building was the tallest structure west of the Mississippi, Baltimore Street leading up to it was still being leveled.

An intriguing blend of restoration and progress marks the city. The urban renaissance has brought modern row houses back to downtown's Quality Hill, the city's most upscale neighborhood over a century ago when it overlooked bustling stockyards and railyards to the west.

Uncommonly affordable housing puts single-family homes within the reach of many who could not buy houses in other metropolitan areas of comparable size. Good prices and good roads for easy commuting continue to contribute to the rapid development of suburban areas, such as Overland Park, Kansas (above).

Early German immigrants gathered at Henry Helmreich's brewery to sample the beers he made with spring water bubbling up through the limestone bluff at 24th and Main. Soon Henry opened the Bellevue Beer Garden on the site (later Signboard Hill and today Crown Center). Martin Keck, his son-in-law, expanded the brewery into Kansas City's first amusement park, the Tivoli Gardens, in 1878. On Sundays German families flocked to the Tivoli for beer, dancing, concerts and carriage rides. Ultimately, Sunday "blue laws" put an end to the Tivoli, for a beer garden without beer was no fun, and a six-day work week left only Sunday for leisure.

One of the city's oldest buildings still in commercial use is Kelly's, a popular bar at the corner of Pennsylvania and Westport Road. Built in 1836 as a tavern by Chief Joseph Walker, the establishment was bought sometime after 1838 by A. G. Boone. The outfitters' station later became the Wiedenmann grocery (shown here about 1906).

Kansas City, Missouri, and Strawberry Hill, the Serbo-Croation community in Kansas City, Kansas. Many families in Independence, Missouri, go back to the first period of settlement soon after 1825.

Still, many once-distinct neighborhoods have disappeared. The residential patterns of the city changed dramatically in the boom years between the Civil War and the new century. Newcomers arrived in droves and the population grew at a rate double that of the nation's.

By the turn of the century, neighborhoods were defined by economics rather than traditions. Automobiles created true suburban life and gave residents the freedom to choose a lifestyle not dependent on proximity to workplaces, businesses and stores. No matter where they lived, people who settled in Kansas City shared and inclination to hard work and a desire for success on their own terms.

It began with the traders and trappers, the area's first businesspeople, who were enticed here by reports from the Lewis and Clark expedition and the ready transportation the rivers offered. In addition to the rivers, the land routes to the West and Southwest brought goods and travelers to the area. Outfitting stations served those headed west. The rich river bottoms attracted farmers. Many pioneers who tried "sod bustin'" and found the prairie so hard it broke their plows came back to Western Missouri. They cut and sold timber, then farmed the rich land that was left. Agriculture flourished, as did livestock production, slaughter and sales.

In 1821 William Becknell, a debtor desperate to evade his creditors, took supplies packed on mules 800 miles overland to Santa Fe, New Mexico, to sell. He returned within the year carrying Mexican silver and reports of eager buyers. From then on Santa Fe trading was a steady opportunity for success, with profits as high as 1,000 percent on the notions, whiskey, tobacco and other goods wagon trains could carry. Trail traders and outfitters flourished, and their commerce

The Kansas City Stockyards Company was organized by 1870. In the river bottoms west of downtown Kansas City, companies such as the giant packing firm of Plankington and Armour opened packing plants. The "Bottoms" became a major transshipment area for beef to Chicago, creating jobs and boosting commerce locally. As a result, the "Kansas City Steak" became famous nationwide by the turn of the century.

The livestock and meatpacking industries flourished until World War II. Ironically, rail transportation built the industry, but another kind of transportation — trucking — ultimately killed it. Trucking gave farmers cheap and easy access to the marketplace and changed the beef industry completely. Today the stockyards are almost silent. Still, local restaurateurs see to it that diners looking for the city's legendary steak are never disappointed.

A fundamental Midwestern work ethic keeps people in every arena dedicated to a job well done. At Stephenson's Apple Orchard (left), fruit for the fall crop is graded and sorted. Agriculture is a complex industry here. More than just farming, it includes the manufacture and sale of equipment, chemicals and fertilizers; trading in commodities and futures; and management of agribusiness enterprises. After a different kind of afternoon's work, firefighters (above) from the Kansas City, Missouri Fire Department cool down.

Never an all-work-no-play kind of town, Kansas City has always prized music and other arts. Choral music has rich local traditions such as the annual presentation of Handel's Messiah. The event, which features the Kansas City Symphony and 500 singers, attracts a sell-out crowd each year to the vast, beautiful Auditorium in the world headquarters of the Reorganized Church of Jesus Christ of the Latter Day Saints in Independence, Missouri. The 110-rank, 6,000-pipe Aeolian-Skinner organ in the Auditorium is one of the largest church organs in the United States.

Many beautiful churches and synagogues in the greater Kansas City area, such as this Greek Orthodox church in Strawberry Hill, recall the ethnic and spiritual heritages of the people who settled here.

attracted more business and settlers, mostly to the towns of Independence, Missouri, and the little crossroads platted in 1835 as Westport, four miles south of the rocky river landing dubbed the Town of Kansas in 1838.

The early Town of Kansas made little pretense of civilization. It was a rough frontier stop, used primarily by Indian traders, mountain men and the overland outfitters. The town had such a reputation for lawlessness that self-respecting outlaws were said to pass it by for tamer places.

Then, just as today, Kansas City was notable for its economic diversity. Livestock, milling, manufacturing, processing, distribution, professions and services of every kind provided the city a broad economic base.

Even when Civil War temporarily put a stop to real growth, the area's business leaders continued to dream of what might come next. There were many possibilities to consider, but they believed that railroads would be the first order of business after the war.

They were right. Kansas City was positioned for explosive change following the war, thanks in great measure to the city's successful bid to have the first rail bridge over the Missouri River. The Hannibal Bridge and the number of rail lines it helped converge here made Kansas City a transportation hub. Beef, brought from Texas and points west, became a major industry, followed by wheat. By 1880 Kansas City was the second largest city after San Francisco in the western half of the United States.

Transportation and commercial distribution created more growth and encouraged new industries, from garments to steel and petroleum. Talented entrepreneurs started companies of many kinds at the end of the old century and beginning of the new. They created new measures of success in fields such as greeting cards, insurance and communications. Residential and commercial development also took innovative directions with the construction of some of the nation's earliest planned residential neighborhoods and shopping areas.

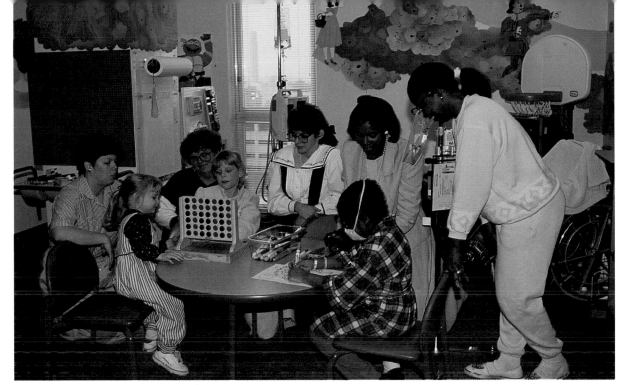

Children's Mercy Hospital was established in 1897 by sisters Dr. Alice Berry Graham, a dentist, and Dr. Katherine Berry Richardson, a physician. Originally dedicated to helping crippled children, the hospital now provides state-of-the-art pediatric medical care of all kinds regardless of the parents' or guardians' ability to pay.

For the annual Children's Mercy Golf Classic, professional golf legend and Kansas City native Tom Watson (above) helps bring other famous golf professionals to the tournament benefitting the hospital.

The first PGA tour stop in Kansas City since 1960 was the Southwestern Bell Senior Classic (left) in 1991, held at the new Loch Lloyd Country Club near Belton, Missouri as a benefit for Crittenton. Galleries of more than 85,000 spectators delighted the PGA which plans future stops in the area. Also delighted were supporters of Crittenton, a comprehensive, non-profit, private mental health organization founded in Kansas City in 1896. Crittenton operates programs in Kansas and Missouri in problem prevention and treatment services for children and families.

Access to a full life for its citizens is the mark of a livable city. Kansas Citians historically have worked to provide it in a number of areas, including many social and sporting activities. Wheelchair athletes (above) participate in the annual Hospital Hill Run which attracts thousands of amateur athletes, including nationally ranked competitors from other cities.

The Kansas City spirit takes to the streets in many forms. Each year for a wild weekend, downtown streets are turned into basketball courts as hundreds of amateur men's and women's teams face off in tournament play.

The Crash of 1929 and its aftermath made for hard times, but less so here since few local businesspeople were speculators. In general, business went on with comparatively little interruption. Because of its varied economic base, Kansas City has traditionally been able to weather downturns in the overall economy better than many cities, and the Great Depression was no exception.

World War II brought dramatic change. War contracts stimulated new and existing industrial enterprises. Business leaders travelled to Washington to argue that the Midwest offered cheap fuels, eager labor, ample raw materials, ready transportation and an inland location safe from enemy attacks. They returned with ordnance, manufacturing, research and communications opportunities that shaped a new direction for Kansas City.

In the years after the war, industrial advances continued along with expansion in other sectors and some important shifts in emphasis for the area. More recently, the area's central location took on new importance as the region became a national hub for telecommunications. Retail and commercial trade has continued to be a pivotal industry, and the region has grown as an important national distribution point that offers bright promise for global importing and exporting.

The development of business in the area is a reflection of the character of the people who live and work here. Vigorous, hardy and hopeful, reliable and productive, they are people for whom work is a guiding principle. Always a city that prized enterprise, Kansas City once levied a tax on loafers. More recently, a multinational insurance company moved its headquarters here when it found that it took only 65 people locally to accomplish the work of 100 on the East coast.

Yet, however industrious, these are not somber folk. It is always easy to attract a crowd in Kansas City, and festivals and celebrations abound. Indeed, Kansas City, Kansas, has drawn on its rich ethnic traditions to build a colorful reputation as the "City of Festivals."

Barbeque (below right), backyards, good buddies and baseball are central to summer life in the area. Literally thousands of teams take the field (above) each year from the World Series-class Kansas City Royals to suburban T-ball leagues for the smallest would-be stars.

In this city of contrasts, tradition and foresight happily blend, as do rural and urban attitudes and activities. This mix is easy to see when the American Royal parade (right) fills the downtown streets. The annual parade kicks off two weeks of rodeos, livestock and horse shows, attracting thousands of spectators and exhibitors.

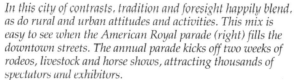

From the blues to bebop, the contribution of Kansas City musicians has been legendary. The annual blues festival draws music-makers and fans nationwide.

(above) The Italian Renaissance setting of the Rozzelle Court in the Nelson-Atkins Museum of Art is a wonderful place to have lunch or an afternoon treat. Under the gallery of the court are exquisite ceiling panels painted in the Renaissance manner by Kansas City artist Daniel MacMorris.

(right) More than 150,000 enthusiasts turn out each year for the annual St. Patrick's Day parade, the second largest in the nation after New York's.

From the beginning, the inclination to gather for play has been a part of the area's history. Some of the first written records of activity in the area are entries in Father Donnelly's journals dated during the 1840s in which the town's first Catholic priest described parties and dances hosted by the Chouteau family. Everyone in the French settlement gathered for hearty stews and foot-stomping fiddle-playing.

Parties even played a role in Kansas City's earliest official naming. A small group of pioneer real estate developers gathered in 1838 to decide what to call the new town. They fell to passing a jug and arguing about whose name the river port should bear. They eventually compromised by choosing the name Kansas, derived from the Kanza Indians, a nearby tribe well-known for feasting, dancing, speechmaking and gambling — all activities the group admired. The place was incorporated as the Town of Kansas (or Kanzas).

More than a hundred and fifty years later, this combination of hard work and hearty play still exists, part of a frontier value system that has survived as a way of life here. Perhaps the two most important of these values are fortitude and what might be called "neighborliness."

Fortitude combines courage with perseverance and flatly refuses to let adversity undo plans for a grander future. Neighborliness is a barn-raising energy, the readiness to help one another build a future together. Together they are the basis of the Kansas City spirit.

This spirit came to the rescue as floods and other disasters tested the mettle of settlers and later residents. Cholera, grasshoppers, border war, civil war and a host of lesser evils repeatedly challenged the fledgling community. At times the rivers helped build the city; in other times they destroyed it. Floods swept away the early French settlement on the Missouri. In 1844, again in 1903 and in 1951, water devastated much of the downtown and

The Mexican-American community on Kansas City's West Side is widely known for its fiestas, especially the Feast of Our Lady of Guadalupe. These traditions are shared with the community at large through appearances by talented folk dance troupes at festivals around the city.

No city parade would be complete without the Marching Cobras, an internationally praised, black coed drill team for urban youth. Founded in 1970 as an after school activity, the Cobras are considered by many to be one of the world's most accomplished drill teams. They have performed in the Presidential Rose Garden and won top honors at the "City of Carnivals Festival" in Nice, France.

Native Americans ranged over the region hunting and fishing until 1825 when the government forced the Kanza and Osage tribes to give up their land along the Missouri River and move to designated areas in Kansas. In the early 1830s, the federal Indian Removal Act drove more eastern tribes into this region, including the Shawnee, Kickapoo, Delaware, Iowa, Sac, Wyandot, Pottawatomie and others. Their tribal names survive as familiar place-names today. The Kansas City Native American population now represents 57 tribes from all over the country. Tribal culture is preserved and shared through powwows and other celebrations throughout the year.

For years, the city was at the mercy of the very rivers that also sustained its early commerce. After the 1903 flood inundated the West Bottoms, bringing business and travel to a halt, the city decided to move Union Depot from Union Street (above) to higher ground. Ten years later, the new Union Station on Pershing Road was almost ready for train traffic, safe from rising water.

Kansas City has come to be recognized for its quality of life and its decent people. In good times and bad, the people of this region keep a steady commitment to sustaining values and traditions.

the livestock and manufacturing businesses in the West Bottoms. Every time, people pitched in and rebuilt — together.

This Kansas City spirit was seen in one of the city's greatest triumphs — its first convention hall. When it opened in 1899, at a cost more than double the original estimates, it was completely debt-free because citizens had donated the funds. Early in 1900, the Democrats chose Kansas City as the site of their national convention that year. Excitement in the city ran high at the thought of the favorable national attention the event promised.

On April 4, however, fire destroyed the hall just three months before the delegates were to arrive. Within hours, the city cabled the Democratic National Committee, "We will have a Convention Hall by July 4." Donations poured in. Masons, carpenters and steelworkers worked day and night. Railroad shipments of materials were put on priority schedules, bumping passengers and goods so that the construction workers could have all they needed to finish "the 90-day miracle." And finish they did, adding the final touches as the first delegates arrived. In the celebration that followed, the phrase "Kansas City Spirit" was coined.

Other challenges, both natural and political, have called this spirit forth repeatedly over the years. Former City Manager L. P. Cookingham observed, "When you talk about a 'Kansas City Spirit,' you are talking about a willingness to give to the city and a willingness on the part of the people to participate in civic improvement."

Early settlers here knew how difficult living and working alone could be. From the beginning, they saw the value of cooperation and the strength in community. They formed ethnic organizations to hold on to their heritages; churches and synagogues to share religious beliefs; benevolent organizations to counter poverty and disease; commerce clubs to encourage economic development; and social clubs for fun.

In the best sense of the phrase, Kansas City

A study in contrasts between old and new (right), Kansas City is still a young city and, in many ways, a young person's city. Teenage visitors at the Westin Crown Center Hotel (above) discover why people-watching is often a sightseer's favorite activity. Youth sports (below) draw big crowds and avid fans. In the fall, Friday night throughout the metroplex is virtually reserved for high school football.

When the 1951 flood devastated the city, Hallmark Cards' founder Joyce C. Hall asked artist Norman Rockwell to create an inspiring image to help strengthen the city during the rebuilding that lay ahead. Rockwell toured the flood sites, talking with citizens, then painted "Kansas City Spirit," which shows some of the city's lasting strengths — transportation, industry, agriculture, fine buildings — and in the foreground, a man rolling up his sleeves for the tasks ahead.

Voluntarism is strong here with hundreds of helping agencies staffed largely by volunteers. Volunteer Action Centers pair willing workers with social needs. Volunteers with Habitat for Humanity (above) build houses in the inner city.

has been a true "melting pot" where many different people have joined together to get things done. This cooperative spirit was described by business leader August Meyer, when he addressed the Commercial Club in Kansas City in 1892 on the topic "How to Build Up a Great City." He spoke of stages of development and personal responsibility for action. He called upon his listeners to display "citizenship in the true and noble sense of the term, which knows no higher aim, nobler ambition, than the greatness, the beauty and the welfare of the city."

Meyer's words voiced the fusion of spirit of place and of people that has occurred here. The city may hold many voices, many desires, but they all come together in a shared vision: Kansas City is a wonderful place to live; *quality of life* is the standard by which this regional city measures itself.

Within that vision, as with the dream that first brought settlers here, can still be seen the land holding forth its silent promise of *better* and *more*, the natural richness of a special place beckoning and a people answering with one voice: *Home.*

Frontier skills persist in a variety of forms, among them a dedication to craft. Despite industrial and technological sophistication, skilled handiwork has a special place in the heartland. Craft shows and fairs are frequent, well-attended events.

Summer in the heartland sends people looking for water, and thousands of visitors find it at Oceans of Fun, a water recreation park in Clay County.

The 1985 World Series was more than baseball. It set the Kansas City Royals against the St. Louis Cardinals, and a long-standing cross-state rivalry added to the fans' fervor. Kansas City gave a heroes' parade for the winning Royals.

Friendly, hard-working, plain-speaking people are the rule in this region where old-fashioned values are prized and old-fashioned heroes revered. National Park Service personnel await visitors in front of the Harry S Truman home in Independence, now open to the public. The former President lived in the house all his married life with his wife, Bess, and they raised their daughter, Margaret, there. It was home; the family viewed their time in Washington as a duty to their country, not an ambition fulfilled. Truman led the nation out of World War II with his "buck stops here" decisiveness and his philosophy of plain-dealing, but local people who knew him well are most likely to recall the way he stood by his friends, cherished his family and loved a game of penny-ante poker.

17

(right) Farmers followed the trappers and traders who were the first settlers here at the beginning of the nineteenth century. Landowners were drawn by the varied terrain with sparkling streams for mills, navigable rivers, tall timber, rich bottomland and rolling upland meadows that promised a good life.

"Most Unforgettable Sight" on many visitors' and residents' lists is a heartland sunset (above and above left) when wide horizons and serene light throw trees and landforms into tender relief. Long springs and late falls make possible an enormous variety of trees and flowers. More than 130 kinds of trees from spruce to magnolia grace the city's celebrated parks and boulevards and the surrounding countryside.

(right) Our identity as a community is partly shaped by shared celebrations. A Fourth of July fireworks display can be seen for miles, and in those moments, myriad watchers in many neighborhoods feel themselves citizens of a true regional city.

Beauty

Who in Europe,
or in America for that matter,
knows that Kansas City is one of
the loveliest cities on earth? ....
Few cities have been built with
so much regard for beauty.

André Maurois
French author

A Magical Mix

The Northland Fountain is a testament to cooperation between public and private sectors and the ability of determined citizens to get things done. Dedicated in 1983 at Vivion Road and North Oak Trafficway, the fountain has operated year-round in Anita B. Gorman Park; in winter its water jets create constantly changing ice sculptures.

(opening) The spectacular Laura Conyers Smith Municipal Rose Garden in Loose Park is one of the city's treasures. Dedicated in 1938, the garden was created by the Kansas City Rose Society and developed by many individuals and groups such as the Kansas City Gardens Association.

(right) Two spectators take in the evening light at Clark Point at 8th and Jefferson. Although Lewis and Clark evidently stopped here in 1806, the point was actually named in 1933 for a former city councilman, Charles H. Clark.

Take an afternoon in Kansas City, at the point high above the rivers where Lewis and Clark stopped on their way west. Pick one of those days in spring when the light seems to come from everywhere at once, palpable, multidimensional — light you can hear and feel and smell almost as much as see.

On such days, Kansas City light can be like the illumination of some nineteenth-century landscape painting in which everything, far and near, appears to be in focus, all of it seen at once: field and farm, highways and rails and rivers, shining steel, glittering glass and cobbled brick, smokestacks and shops, all equally immediate. When the light is that way, and one has time and a place high enough to look about, the effect is remarkable. For an instant, *here* reaches to the encircling horizon. *Here* seems to be everywhere.

Visitors are usually amazed by the simple beauty of this region. It has an unassuming loveliness, not dependent on any dominant feature. No crashing sea, no soaring peaks, no single topographical feature unique enough to be known to strangers by name, the way people know Seattle's Mt. Rainier or Boston's harbor. Instead, Kansas City is beautiful in the combination of its elements, natural and built. Sojourners see it fresh and are enchanted.

Residents see it routinely and forget how special it is until our eyes are somehow drawn to it again. Showing the city to a visitor can renew appreciation of the area's beauty. Sometimes something we've loved is lost in our cityscape and the loss makes us acutely aware of what remains. If a giant neighborhood sycamore is felled by a storm, we see at once not only the lost beauty of the tree but *all*

the neighborhood, leaf and brick and bloom, in dear detail.

At these times, we glimpse the true interconnectedness of people and their surroundings. We see that the beauty of an area is a sum of many very different parts, each contributing to a working harmony that is more than the appearance of a place. It is its character.

A real place is not just a habitation, it is a place to abide. What makes Kansas City a real place is all but impossible to put into words, like many of the other best mysteries of life. But some things can be documented:

· extraordinary topography and geophysical features
· a genuine regional character
· varied and humane architecture
· a vital and splendidly planned parks and boulevards system
· superb residential district design and space
· a multicultural population that contributes many different expressions of beauty.

Anyone who expects Kansas City to be flat and corn-rowed is caught off guard by its hilliness. Elevation ranges from 72 feet to 1,105 feet above sea level. Even though early settlers leveled hills and carved through bluffs to create what is now downtown Kansas City, Missouri, the essentially rolling character of the land is unchanged, shaped by water and ice millennia ago and by wind and water since.

The natural landscape is a study in contrasts. Characteristics of four distinct geophysical regions mingle here. Flat bottomland along the river presses against bluffs to the east and south. Open prairie runs away to the

Some hardy families came to the Kansas Territory when it officially opened in 1854, but the real land rush began with the Homestead Act of 1862. The act gave 160 acres to any citizen 21 years old who had a $10 filing fee and the grit to improve the land for five years. The only natural resources were blazing sun, fertile soil and grass for grazing animals. One pioneer woman wrote that when she arrived on the plains as a child, her father showed her "something very precious — a plow. . . it was to be our means of support. Not a single tree was there; just bare prairie." From that prairie came the crops that made Kansas City one of the world's great agricultural capitals.

west from the hills along the border between Missouri and Kansas. Rocky underpinnings show from cuts in the hills and create jagged slashes beneath soft swells of green. Stands of timber punctuate meadows. And there is water, in a surprising number of rivers, countless streams, lakes and ponds — so many bodies of water that from the air they glitter like the scattered shards of a giant's broken mirror.

The soil is rich and — like so much else in the region — full of the unexpected. Scientists say only 11 percent of the surface of the planet is ideal for growing food. Much of that percentage is in North America, and much of *that* is close by the Kansas City region.

The fertile earth is complemented by a varied climate that encourages an astonishing horticultural mix: blueberries, azaleas, cactus and spruce grow with nearly equal success. The region seems to borrow from every climate imaginable: long, moist springs; hot summers; slow, crisp falls; cold, sometimes blustery winters. Kansas City weather is terrific for growing trees, inspiring calendar-makers and exciting children — but can be tough on forecasters. Like its geographic features, climatic areas meet in Kansas City with sometimes abrupt and dramatic results.

While the fertile land and flowing waters may have seemed like unbridled opportunity to early settlers, the landforms posed serious challenges to some town builders. Parts of the region offered fairly accessible town sites — Independence, Missouri, and Shawnee, Kansas, come to mind — where water was plentiful but floods unlikely, and the land-scape was flat enough to accommodate road-building. Tidy four-cornered towns grew up in such places as these.

But the new Town of Kansas had none of those advantages. It was sited at both the top and bottom of bluffs along the Missouri River, without viable space for streets or building lots. Stores and homes clung to hillsides or rode precariously on top, vulnerable to mudslides or to wind. Most early buildings were haphazard

and graceless, long flat warehouses for business or huddles of huts for residential areas.

Later, however, immigrants began to bring to the city Eastern expectations of style. These were translated into a building spree that gave Kansas City a growing architectural reputation as the "Athens of the West." By the late 1880s, residents had built the third-largest train station in the world, the Union Depot at Ninth and Union streets in the West Bottoms. They modelled the fanciful "Crystal Palace" agricultural exposition center after a similar glass building erected in London for Queen Victoria. And they constructed the luxurious Coates House Hotel and Coates Opera House.

During the last two decades of the 19th century, such significant buildings began setting an architectural tone for the city. Many followed the national taste of the times for ornamentation and neo-Gothic styling. Other buildings showed a modern simplicity of line that foreshadowed twentieth-century building.

But already beginning — and fueled by the wild land speculations of the 1880s — was a trend to abandon developed areas for new commercial or residential areas. "Knobs," as the wealthy residents of one part of town were known, moved into even grander houses along Independence Avenue. Quality Hill homes were left behind for tonier mansions in Hyde Park. A new commercial and retail center built up around 11th and Grand, drawing customers away from the older City Market.

Coupled with the fact that no building codes or zoning ordinances regulated growth, this build-and-move approach created a random development sprawl. Areas were in use only a few years, then fell into decline. The real estate bust of the early 1890s added to the disorder, leaving properties abandoned and residential developments unfinished, their connecting streetcar rails rusting from disuse. In less than half a century, the splendid wilderness had turned into an ironic blend of progress and poor planning.

No wonder that the issue of "quality of life" became a rallying cry in the 1890s. Within

Favorable winds and gorgeous topography make the region a treat for hot-air balloonists.

Spring one day, snow the next. Gardeners keep a close watch on frost until late April.

No wonder New England settlers felt at home here. Kansas City has its own flaming fall revue.

On some autumn evenings, the wild cries of migrating geese can be heard over the sounds of the city. Flying wedges of Canada geese are a familiar sign of fall because the Kansas City region is on the birds' north/south flyway.

Boom-and-bust years in the late 1880s meant immigrants found a depressed economy and few jobs. Many of them stayed in shantytowns that cascaded down hills near prosperous neighborhoods. Cleaning up the West Bluffs (here seen from 13th in about 1892) was a key point in the first parks and boulevards plan; the area became the beautiful West Terrace Park. Today highway expansion has taken most of the original park, although the stone outlook remains.

the next quarter century, the phrase would find expression in two forces for change that would converge to shape Kansas City's environment for the remainder of the twentieth century. These forces were the parks and boulevards movement and the emergence of the planned residential and shopping community. They represented the gathered energies of some extraordinarily visionary individuals and the hard work of great numbers of committed citizens.

When William Rockhill Nelson moved to Kansas City from Indiana in 1880 he was appalled to find unpaved streets and no sidewalks beyond the rough boards some merchants laid before their doors. Soon after he bought his paper, the *Kansas City Evening Star,* he set to work to stir up change, and he didn't spare the whip. "Individuals profit by judicious and liberal expenditures of money," he wrote. "So do cities. Kansas City has reached a point where she must make expenditures if she is to occupy the proud position within her reach. The pinching economy, the picayunish policy, the miserable parsimony, which characterizes our city government must now be abandoned or the city's growth will be seriously retarded and her best interest greatly crippled."

A year later, he moved beyond his crusade for better fire protection and street lamps, and focused on public recreation and parks. The gospel of the great nineteenth-century park designers such as Frederick L. Olmsted was being heard in many cities: parks were essential to a civilized and productive city. Nelson carried the idea like a banner.

In the beginning and for several years, his opposition was stiff and vocal. They included enormously powerful public figures, among them Louis Hammerslough, a German immigrant who had made a fortune selling clothes. He sold his business in the 1880s and bought the local German-language newspaper, which he used to express his views, many of them aggressively against a park system. Colonel Thomas H. Swope, a wealthy Inde-

pendence recluse with considerable Kansas City property holdings, fought Nelson's plans because he believed the cost of building parks would be levied against city landowners as increased taxes. And James Reed, later a United States Senator, was accused by the *Star* of trying to wreck the parks plan.

Ironically, however, these three eventually became champions of the parks and boulevards system. Hammerslough was one of the first park board commissioners. Reed, elected mayor in 1900, oversaw four of the most productive years of the system's development. And Swope gave the city the largest gift of land in its history, before or since, when he provided a 1,334-acre tract of land four miles from downtown on the condition that the land be used as a public park forever.

Gradually the opposition was overridden by the efforts of Nelson, Kersey Coates, Robert Gillham, Adriance Van Brunt, S. B. Armour, and, perhaps most important, August W. Meyer, a smelting magnate and nature lover. Meyer had known a young landscape architect, George Kessler, who had come to the area with a commission to design a railroad park in Merriam, Kansas. The German-born Kessler had been educated in the tradition of great European parks, and he brought to Kansas City the idea that a parks and boulevards system could provide a central element to unify and beautify a city.

After several attempts by the city to organize a park board, one finally was established in 1891. George Kessler promptly presented his credentials. The board had little funding and no legal means to raise money, so funds for landscape architects were limited. But George Kessler was so drawn to the work itself that he accepted a position as secretary to the board for $100 a month and agreed to serve as engineer for no additional salary.

Kessler began to design and, in 1893, presented the park board with a plan that came to exemplify the City Beautiful movement that was taking hold in the nation's more sophisticated cities. Kessler's plan used

After a rain, Brush Creek runs full through the Country Club Plaza, foreshadowing the ambitious project now under way to develop the creek from State Line Road to the Blue River into a lock-controlled watercourse with lakes, small boats, streamside walkways and cultural areas, including cafes, outdoor seating and an amphitheater.

The Spirit of Freedom Fountain, with its sculpture by Richard Hunt, commemorates contributions of the black population in Kansas City and its leaders past and present, particularly the fountain project's initiator, Bruce R. Watkins.

The landmark Verona Columns were brought from Italy for a park in Mission Hills, Kansas in 1925.

Columns at Gregory Boulevard and Ward Parkway are representative of the art that graces public places throughout the city.

the best of Beaux Arts ideas about grand, classical architecture, serene vistas and public promenades. But the plan also celebrated what Kessler called "the eccentricities of topography" in the area. Boulevards curved along hills. The wild beauty of gorges and rocky bluffs was incorporated into roadways ideal for scenic hikes or drives. Altogether, the original plan called for boulevards — adapted to traffic patterns for the automobile, a contraption already fascinating the public — to hold together a system of parks throughout the city. The boulevards would attract fine homes; parks would guarantee residents green space.

An amendment to the city charter in 1895 gave the park board administrative power and fiscal independence. An innovative plan to sell "park certificates" to financial institutions permitted immediate funding, and early construction was quickly under way. The original plan was complete by 1915, and Kansas City had its first and perhaps most lastingly unique feature — a parks and boulevards system of unrivaled beauty that influenced city planners throughout the nation.

Already, a young real estate developer was building along the southern edge of the boulevards in Kessler's plan. In 1905, J. C. Nichols bought 10 acres of land at about 51st Street and Grand Avenue along Brookside Boulevard.

Nichols was influenced by the charm of European villages clustered around a group of shops. He built Crestwood, a small shopping area at 55th and Oak, to serve his residences and to create a buffer against sub-standard merchant establishments. He laid out curving streets that sometimes purposely wound hither and yon to save large trees that might otherwise have been in the roadbuilders' path. He sited homes on generous lots that kept the existing terrain as unchanged as possible.

Although success came swiftly to him in the form of sturdy suburbs of solid middle-class homes, he began to envision building something grander: an "Arcadia for

Homebuilding." That's how promotional material described Mission Hills with its walkways, rills, falls, ponds and reflecting pools, copses, ornamental flower beds, meadows and other delights of the nineteenth-century landscaper's art. Although the early large estates have been broken into smaller lots now, throughout Mission Hills, Kansas some of these landscape elements remain and continue to give to the area much of the grace Nichols imagined.

In Mission Hills and in his other developments, Nichols set examples that were followed by developers all over the metropolitan area and in other parts of the country. He worked closely with Kessler protégé, Sid Hare, and his son Herbert, as Hare & Hare laid out street plans for his developments. To assure that homes would live up to their neighborhoods' standards and keep resale value over several generations, he pioneered the use of deed restrictions and homes associations dedicated to the upkeep and beautification of the area. Today homes associations are a vital part of the life of neighborhoods all over the metro area, indeed, all over America.

Owning a home has always been important to the independent-minded settlers of the region. Kansas City long has had one of the highest percentages of homeownership among similarly sized cities in the country. In addition, ideas about gardens and trees put into residential practice during the early suburban growth years have influenced developers ever since. Today's leisure communities, built around golf courses and lakes, and the expectation of most suburban dwellers that they will have a substantial lot to landscape as they wish, are all legacies from this crucial era of residential planning.

From the beginning, Kansas City recognized itself as a "work in progress" and willingly looked elsewhere for help in growing. Business owners and others did not hesitate to bring in nationally recognized architects and landscape architects such as Stanford White (of New York's McKim, Mead

On the grounds of the Nelson-Atkins Museum of Art, an original casting of Auguste Rodin's "The Thinker" makes a place to take one's bearings.

For a few days each spring, migration brings the monarch butterflies, a royal presence in fields and gardens.

The J.C. Nichols Memorial Fountain (47th and J.C. Nichols Parkway in Mill Creek Park) is the best-known, best-loved and most frequently photographed fountain in the city. Brought from a Long Island estate, the fountain was dedicated in 1960. Today it anchors Mill Creek Park, developed through private and public funding into a much-used exercise park, and provides a handsome counterpoint to the Giralda Tower at the north end of the Country Club Plaza.

At the Burr Oak Woods Nature Center in Blue Springs, Missouri, visitors meet nature face to face. The park is one of the region's several wildlife refuge areas, such as the James A. Reed Memorial Wildlife Area, also in Jackson County, and the Martha Lafite Thompson Nature Sanctuary in Liberty, Missouri.

The Kansas City Zoo is located in Swope Park (Swope Parkway and Meyer Boulevard), the second-largest city park in the country.

From the beginning, the region's fine homes reflected a range of architectural styles and combinations, from the splendid excess of mansions such as Mineral Hall (top), named for the decorative minerals in its arched entrance and now part of the Kansas City Art Institute, to the tidy "shirtwaist" homes (below) built by the hundreds in the early twentieth century. Named for ladies' white blouses and dark skirts — and often said to be Kansas City's only truly original home style — traditional shirtwaist houses had a light stucco upper floor and brick or stone first floor. Prized today by restorers in older neighborhoods, they are often imaginatively revitalized in other color combinations.

& White) and George Kessler. The relatively steady building that went on from the 1880s to the 1960s attracted architects and planners who made significant contributions to the area's architecture. Among the best known were: Frank Lloyd Wright, who designed the Community Christian Church (4601 Main); Louis S. Curtiss, who designed the Folly Theater (300 West 12th) and the Bernard Corrigan residence (1200 West 55th); Nelle E. Peters, the city's first female architect, who designed hundreds of apartment buildings including the James Russell Lowell (722 Ward Parkway); Walter C. Root and George M. Siemens (Root & Siemens), who designed the Scarritt Building (818 Grand) and the Country Club Congregational Church (205 West 65th); and Edward Larrabee Barnes, who was the original master planner and coordinating architect for Crown Center (2450 Grand).

The city is especially renowned for buildings in the Art Deco style; many architectural historians regard the Power and Light Building (1330 Baltimore), the City Hall (414 East 12th), the Jackson County Courthouse (415 East 12th) and the Municipal Auditorium (13th and Wyandotte) as among the best examples in the world of the clean, stylized and streamlined forms of Art Deco architecture.

During the 1970s and 1980s, commercial growth and concentrated efforts by the area's developers to strengthen the commercial infrastructure resulted in several billion dollars worth of new construction. Hundreds of new office buildings were built, and on the downtown Kansas City, Missouri skyline exciting new structures pushed at the sky. Many of these reflected the quest for architectural excellence and superior craftsmanship that had distinguished earlier buildings in the region.

Equally exciting developments occurred in the suburbs where contemporary office parks such as Corporate Woods in Overland Park, Kansas, integrated offices into the landscape to provide workers a pleasing and productive mix of designed and natural

environments. The mixed-use development — offices, residences and shops designed as a functioning whole — has made an increasingly important contribution not only to the pace of life in Kansas City, but also to its visual landscape.

The most successful and best-known mixed-use development is Crown Center, which opened in 1973. It was conceived in the 1960s by Joyce C. Hall, founder of Hallmark Cards, Inc., and his son, Donald J. Hall, the current chairman of the board. From the start, it was meant to be a city-within-a-city at the heart of the metropolitan area. Crown Center is an outstanding mix of offices, shops, restaurants, theaters and apartments that marries natural and designed beauty to meet the many needs and desires of people, from privacy for daily living to space for public celebrations.

Plans for the future will only further this kind of special integration and make the downtown region lovelier and more usable. Soon to come is a renovated and expanded City Market area in the old town around 4th Street and ambitious riverfront projects that will recall the heritage and possibilities along both of the region's great rivers. Plans for renovations and additions along Grand Avenue will create an important mixed-use corridor linking downtown, Crown Center and the Country Club Plaza.

And, in the spirit of Kessler and the early planners, the boulevard system will continue to grow with a Centennial Boulevard (celebrating a century of parks and boulevards). It will begin north at the airport, cross the city and end in the south at Jerry Smith Park at 135th. The route has been planned to unite neighborhoods and people throughout the region by providing a continuous drivable link between them all. Much of the intriguing variety of the region has come from the differences people bring to their homes and workplaces. Centennial Boulevard will wind through many different areas, helping residents and visitors alike further appreciate the area's multi-cultural aspects.

Adaptive reuse sparked urban renewal during the 1970s. Through the work of committed organizations and individuals, fine old buildings were brought back into the active business and social life of the community.

In the early 1970s, restoration became a watchword and many of the area's beautiful homes, such as this one on historic Park Street in Olathe, Kansas, became both residences and regional treasures.

Another beautiful residential setting is offered by many lake communities that ring the central city. Weatherby Lake nestles in the wooded hills of Platte County.

After all, much of the beauty of Kansas City springs from unexpected juxtapositions of old and new, big and small, timeless and transitory. The resulting humanized landscape is enormously rich, nourishing the spirit with its diversity.

Kansas City has all these things: urban and rural spaces together; verdant earth, clear air and water in clean and abundant supply; strong, carefully detailed and often joyful built forms. And, perhaps most important, this region invites enjoyment in a hospitable landscape that reveals the basic connection between the land and the people who inhabit it.

Texture, ornament and decoration are everywhere throughout the region, a feast for the eye. Spectacular mosaic tile work is one of the distinguishing characteristics of the Country Club Plaza (right), and a midtown residence is glorified by its details (above). The branches and splashing water of the Rain Thicket Fountain (right) in the Oppenstein Memorial Park at 12th and Walnut enliven a downtown corner.

Contrast creates energy and excitement citywide: the sweep of The Link (above left), the glass walkway connecting the hotels, shops and offices of Crown Center; the Liberty Memorial Frieze (above) on Pershing Road; the rustic beauty of an old mill at Shoal Creek (near left) and an early snowfall against a plaza dome on Ward Parkway (far left).

Summer pleasures include a foggy lane in Clay County (above right) and the Henry Moore Sculpture Garden (above) on the South Lawn of the Nelson-Atkins Museum of Art. The garden, made possible by grants and a long-term loan from the Hall Family Foundations of almost 60 works by Henry Moore, has become one of the area's favorite outdoor spaces since it opened in 1990. Sheep Piece (foreground in photo and so called, Moore has said, because he put it in a field and the sheep liked it) was already on the grounds. The collection comprises the largest presentation of Moore's work outside his native England.

Winter splendors: (above) the bundled serenity of a walk along the Liberty Memorial Mall in the avenue of trees planted in the 1940s by the Navy War Mothers and the Army Mothers Club as memorials to their sons; (right) the dramatic ice break-ups on the Missouri River.

(far right) Jokingly called the "Flashcube" when it was first built, the office building at 95th and Metcalf with its lake and fountain has become an important Johnson County landmark.

Memory

The growth of Kansas City,
taken in connection with the
extent of her resources and commerce,
constitutes a progress that cannot
find a parallel in American history.

Charles Carroll Spalding
Kansas City Journalist
"Annals of the City of Kansas 1858"

Portal to the West

Fort Osage was established on the Missouri River in 1808 as a government trading post. On the strength of its fur trade, the fort became the largest of the government "factories," but in 1822, under pressure from private fur companies, the government closed the fort. That left the Missouri River along present-day Jackson County open for such French fur traders as the Chouteau family. Historical reenactments such as the 1812 Militia Muster draw visitors today to the reconstructed fort.

(opening) In the 1890s, a two-block corridor of shops along 11th from Walnut to Main became known as Petticoat Lane (shown here on a postcard from the era). Ladies shopping there inadvertently showed their petticoats when they lifted their skirts so their hems wouldn't drag as they stepped off the streetcars. Many of the beloved names of Kansas City retailing were there: Peck's; Emery, Bird & Thayer; Rothschild; Harzfelds; and the Jones Store, the only one still in business today.

(right) The Pioneer Mother Memorial, located in Penn Valley Park, is one of Kansas City's best-known statues. It was put in place in 1927 as a tribute to the women settlers who made the arduous journey west.

François Chouteau's trading post was little more than a few log cabins and a warehouse when it was built in 1821. But the first permanent white settlement in the Kansas City area also was a portal to a vast fur-trading empire. Day after day, 75-foot-long, cigar-shaped keelboats slipped away from Chouteau's wharf, stacked high with furs and hides brought there by Indian tribes throughout the plains.

Each year, the boats carried away cargo equal to more than $10 million in today's dollars. So when floods swept away the little village in 1825, the Chouteau family and employees decided business was too good to abandon. They built again on higher ground near what is now Troost Avenue.

It is perhaps the first recorded instance of a habit of mind that characterizes Kansas City history: the willingness to begin important things, to overcome obstacles, then start all over again if necessary. Like the fabled phoenix, the city has risen time and again from what appeared to be certain doom.

That is the character of this region. For thousands of years, nature has given and taken away from all who come here. Yet strong and persevering people have seized a living from this place.

As the great glacier receded north about 10,000 B.C., hunting nomads roamed the area. They left behind stone implements as their only record. While Julius Caesar was busy conquering Gaul, a band of Hopewell Indians made a vigorous settlement along Line Creek in what is now Platte County. By A.D. 800, a culture of Mound Builders had moved into the area. They probably are the primary ancestors of tribes whose names are familiar as regional place-names today: the Missouri, Kanza, Iowa, Osage and Omaha.

Spaniards led by Francisco Vasquez de Coronado rode onto the Kansas plains in the mid-1500s searching for the mythical Seven Cities of Cibola and their riches. The Conquistadors found no golden treasure and went away with little but sketched maps of a vast wilderness. A stone found in the area with the inscription, "August 31 1541 I take for Spain Quivira Francisco" is in the courthouse in Lyons, Kansas.

Like the Spanish, the English claimed land here during the seventeenth and eighteenth centuries, but left few traces of their passage. Only the French made their mark. They used the rivers, which had been the Indians' alone for generations, to explore and to trap. They bartered goods with the tribes and exchanged elements of language and religion.

Etienne Veniard de Bourgmont, generally thought to be the first European to reach the Kansas City area, passed the mouth of the Kaw in 1713. He was surveying the Missouri River, believed at that time to flow west to the Pacific, in the hopes of finding a passage to the western mountains and their rumored silver veins. Although he failed at that attempt, he returned from France ten years later to build Fort Orleans on the Missouri River in what is now Carroll County. The fort was abandoned by 1729, but the French continued to trade up and down the river.

In 1800 Napoleon bought for France land which included Missouri and Kansas. Three years later, he sold the property known as the Louisiana Territory to the United States for $15 million, or about three-and-a-half cents an acre. The sale had no real impact on the

The area platted as the Town of Kansas saw its first American-owned trading house open in 1839. The struggling settlement on the river levee was chartered as the City of Kansas in 1853 and popularly called "Kansas City." The name was made official in 1889. The original town clustered along the river on Levee Street until roads could be blasted through the bluffs and the rough hills cleared for buildings. By the early 1860s (above) some semblance of order was evident, but the War Between the States soon halted progress.

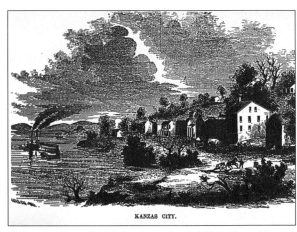

A drawing from the 1850s shows the fledgling City of Kansas with the spelling urged by missionaries (who said the Indians pronounced their name with a "z" sound) and journalists (who wanted to avoid confusion with Arkansas). By 1860, however, the mapmakers' spelling of Kansas had prevailed.

Frenchmen who continued to trap and hunt in the area they called "Chez les Canses," near the mouth of the Kaw.

Right away, President Thomas Jefferson encouraged exploration of the western purchase. By 1803 Captain Meriwether Lewis and Lieutenant William Clark were headed to the northwest. They camped in 1804 on the plain where the Kaw and Missouri met. On their way back through the area two years later, their notes record the observation that the "high hill [above the rivers] has many advantages for a trading house or fort."

Fourteen years later, the ambitious Chouteau family of St. Louis seized the opportunity Lewis and Clark had glimpsed. In 1820 François Chouteau was sent upriver to scout warehouse sites for the American Fur Company, which the Chouteaus hoped to build into a fur monopoly. The rivers' bend seemed ideal for controlling water and land access to the trapping territories.

The Kawsmouth French, as Chouteau's settlement was known, had no desire to colonize and did not try to attract others to join them. Nonetheless, the area quickly became the gathering point for a diverse stream of refugees, visionaries, pioneers and others looking for a place to settle. Their immigration, some by choice, others by force, would greatly influence how the area developed.

At the time Missouri was admitted to the Union in 1821, Nebraska appeared on most maps as "The Great American Desert," and Kansas was called "Indian Territory." Steadily over the next two decades, Kansas became the forced destination for Indians from the upper Mississippi Valley. To make more room for immigrants in Eastern states, Native Americans were "resettled" west of the Missouri state line under a series of treaties that were revised or broken as new land was required for further western expansion.

A number of tribes were relocated here by 1836, including the Iowa, Kickapoo, Delaware, Sauk and Pottawattomie. The federal Indian Agency office was a log cabin situated at the current corner of 59th Street and State Line Road. In what is now Kansas City, Kansas, the Wyandot tribe bought 38 sections of land from the Delaware, and the Shawnee came to a reservation in Northeast Johnson County.

While some settlers were forced into the area, others were led here. Guided by their prophet Joseph Smith's visions and by reports of the region's fertile land, a deputation of the Church of Jesus Christ of the Latter Day Saints arrived in 1831, seeking a site for their New Jerusalem. The church members settled in Independence, Missouri. The town had a post office, a store and two of the essentials of frontier life – a miller to grind meal and a lawyer to arbitrate disputes. Unfortunately, the disputes between mainstream Protestant settlers and the Saints, which were not settled for nearly fifty years, drove Joseph Smith and his followers from the area in 1838. The Reorganized Church of Jesus Christ of the Latter Day Saints (RLDS) began a return to Independence in 1877, and, in 1920, Independence was rededicated by the group as the true Zion.

When Smith's followers first settled in Independence, it was already the seat of a county designated in 1826 and named for war hero Andrew Jackson. There was little river traffic, so a town site was picked about three miles from the river where springs fed clear streams. Although the river later became a greater factor in area commerce, Independence grew more from the needs of overland travelers and the plans of farming families who wanted to move west, but not too far.

In the 1840s families joined the mule drivers, mountain men and merchants at the Independence marketplace. Lured by tales of riches and prosperity in California and Oregon, they came in boats to Independence, then bought supplies and wagons for the 2,000-mile journey. In one instance, 1,000 travelers met at Elm Grove, Missouri, to take the trail together. By the end of the decade, the Oregon Territory had a population of nearly 12,000, and most of them had come through Independence.

The Huron Indian Cemetery located at Seventh and Armstrong in Kansas City, Kansas, served as one of the Wyandot Indians' tribal burial grounds from 1844 to 1959. It became the focus of national attention in 1904 when local commercial interests revealed plans to move the Indian dead and develop the land. Lyda Burton Conley, a Wyandot descendant, and her sister, Floating Voice, occupied the cemetery, threatening to shoot anyone who disturbed the graves. They built and lived in a shack there for six years while Conley studied law and became the first Native American woman lawyer in the United States. In 1910 she took the cemetery case to the U.S. Supreme Court, which refused to interfere with Congress' intent to sell the land. But galvanized by Conley's efforts, women's groups nationally pressured Congress into passing a bill prohibiting removal of the cemetery where the Conley and her sister now are buried. Today it is maintained as a city park.

The first permanent white settler in Wyandotte County was Moses Grinter. He came to the area in 1831 to operate a ferry across the Kansas River near what is now 78th in Kansas City, Kansas. In 1857 he built a two-story house of brick made from clay, river sand and animal hair (for added strength). Now the oldest building in Wyandotte County, the house is open to the public.

People and freight came to town by boat on the Missouri from 1850 until after the Civil War. The blasts of the boats' whistles and the shout "Steamboat's a'comin'" brought people down to the levee even if they were not expecting guests or goods. Boat landings at the foot of Grand (then called Market) or Main (above) were bustling, exciting places to be. Once the railroads were well-established in the early 1870s, steamboat traffic declined and died.

A turning point in the history of the region was the opening of the Hannibal Bridge on July 3, 1869. More than 20,000 people gathered to celebrate the link that made possible the first direct rail line to Chicago — and with it the commercial development of Kansas City. Following a parade, the crowd trooped to the bridge to witness the Hannibal, the pride of the Hannibal and St. Joseph Railroad, steam across the bridge with 10 railcars in tow. The bridge's central span then was pivoted to let a steamboat pass through. The day ended with numerous speeches, a giant barbeque and fireworks.

About 1870, Main looking north from 6th (above) was a study in contrasts. Brick buildings lined muddy streets and an Academy of Music sat opposite the Marble Hall, a favorite gambling spot for Wyatt Earp, Bat Masterson, Buffalo Bill Cody, Wild Bill Hickok and other legends of the West. Gambling was serious business. In a six-block section of Main in the 1870s were more gambling houses than in any other city in America. When the government instituted the Johnson Anti-Gambling Act in 1881, Bob Potee, prince of dealers and owner of the gambling house Faro Number 3 on Missouri Avenue, saw the end of a way of life and (stories say) put on his silk hat and walked north on Main — chatting with everyone he knew — until he walked right into the Missouri River and drowned himself.

Nearby villages prospered too. After the first day's travel out of Independence, pioneers stopped for fresh food and water in Raytown, Missouri. The trail then looped westward through today's Penn Valley Park and on into Kansas toward a spot between Edgerton and Gardner where the road forked and the signs pointed to "Santa Fe" and to "Oregon."

Alert to opportunity, 20-year-old John Calvin McCoy opened a store in 1831. The log building faced the Santa Fe Trail on what would become the corner of Westport Road and Pennsylvania. McCoy had plenty of customers, including Indians and settlers relocating along the states' borders. It wasn't a particularly commanding place, compared to lushly wooded eastern Jackson County farms or fertile rolling land just inside Kansas. But the young merchant had a knack for seeing possibilities where others didn't. He filed a plat in 1835 for a nine-square-block town he called "West Port" because he imagined it would be a portal to the western wilderness.

About four miles north of McCoy's store, on neighbor Gabriel Prudhomme's land, was a rocky river ledge at the foot of what became Grand Avenue. The ledge looked to McCoy like a natural levee and boat landing. When the farm came up for sale in 1838, he formed the Kansas Town Company along with 13 other men and bought the 271 acres. He christened the ledge "Westport Landing," and it substantially shortened the land route that goods had to travel from the river to Westport outfitters' stations. His foresight earned McCoy the nickname "Father of Two Cities," Westport and Kansas City, Missouri.

More than foresight must have been required to tackle building a city on the limestone bluffs above the rivers. Dreams. Visions. Some said hallucinations. A critical eye would have seen only abrupt hills jutting up from land so densely wooded and vined as to be impassable (the vines were a plague for years — today they survive only in the name of world-famous Vine Street).

The Town Company put up warehouses and businesses built from the logs cut as they cleared the hillsides. In 1844, the Missouri River rolled in her bed, the channel shifted and floodwaters completely swept away the Town of Kansas, leaving only Colonel W.M. Chick's warehouse. When the water went down, the settlers built again, this time higher up, using sturdy brick made from the river bottom clay and baked in lime kilns set up by William Weston in 1846.

The village was incorporated as the Town of Kansas in 1850. A special act of the Missouri Legislature chartered the growing community as the City of Kansas three years later. By then Colonel Chick and others had brick homes east of Grand on top of Pearl Hill, later leveled to make way for more growth. Even so, a journalist from Ohio passing through found the fledgling town site "rough and not at all attractive."

Not everyone agreed, however, especially not Chick, who, as the first postmaster, had a post office in one corner of his store on the levee. When Chick heard a steamboat coming, he strolled out under the guise of meeting the mail but, in fact, it was to meet the passengers and to exclaim upon the virtues of the place.

By 1857 the town had 450 businesses, including three harness shops that produced $81,000 worth of tack that year, 40 manufacturers that produced goods valued at more than $330,000, five saw mills, two grain mills, 16 hotels and a busy social life ranging from productions of Shakespeare at Long's Hall to poker in various gambling houses. There also were 26 saloons for 4,400 residents and mud as deep as a man's thigh in streets where pigs ran free.

It was a tough frontier town, virtually lawless in any formal way, but with a code of ethics and clear-cut loyalties quickly made plain to new arrivals or passing strangers. The *Westport Border Star* (the town's second paper, established in 1855) had a stated editorial policy that might well have been the watchword for the entire City of Kansas:

The combination of productive farms and plentiful streams made milling of all kinds important to the nineteenth-century economy of the region. The Watkins Woolen Mill in Lawson, Missouri (above), is one of the few factories in America from that period with its original machinery intact.

Given to the city in 1846 by the William Gillis family to be a public market square, the land at about 5th and Main was developed in 1857 and the City Market has been in operation in the same place ever since. The first prominent public building in the city, at 4th and Main, was a combined city hall and market house. By 1878, farmers crowded the square with wagonloads of produce (above right). In 1892, a new city hall was built on the same site as the old one and was connected by a walkway to market buildings along Walnut (lower right in picture at lower left).

Until the current City Hall was built in 1937, the Market Square was the heart of government and commerce for Kansas City. In 1940, new market buildings were put up and shoppers continued to visit the market (below), especially for fresh produce, poultry and fish, just as they do today.

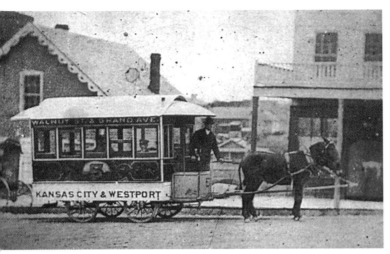

By 1869 the City of Kansas needed public transportation and the Kansas City and Westport Horse Railway Company (above) opened for business. By the mid-1870s horsecars carried passengers south to Westport, west to Kansas City, Kansas, and east to Prospect. A cable railway was introduced in 1885. By 1894 the city had the nation's third-largest cable railway system.

"We know we are right and we go ahead."

It was an attitude needed for the most elementary task at hand: cutting a city out of rock. To succeed, the City of Kansas had to overcome the bluffs that held it captive on Levee Street. Along the river's edge was just enough space for one row of shops. Workmen blasted and cut through layers of stone from the top of the bluffs until they had streets level enough to drive a wagon on; some roads wound up being 50 feet deep between walls of stone. Building owners at the tops of these man-made cliffs remodeled with each blast, adding levels downward to keep an entrance at "street level."

With this same tenacity, city boosters set out to attract new residents. The most skilled at this was probably Robert T. Van Horn, who published the *Journal of Commerce* and books and pamphlets designed to bring Easterners west. With the opening of the Kansas Territory in 1854 and passage of the Homestead Act in 1862, would-be pioneers poured into Kansas City. Van Horn and others convinced many to stay rather than trudge further west.

As more people moved in, bringing their own traditions and beliefs, culture clash was inevitable. During the 1830s and 1840s, many settlers were Southerners attracted by the chance to expand their farming operations in Missouri, where slavery was legal. During the 1850s, more New Englanders and other Easterners arrived. They were supported by the Boston Emigrant Aid Society and other groups that underwrote immigration to the West to further commercial ambitions and to send potential voters to sway Kansas to Free State status.

When the passage of the Kansas-Nebraska Act of 1854 reopened slavery extension as an issue and made Kansas a household word, a widespread debate on the spelling of Kansas Territory arose. The government had declared it *Kansas* despite missionaries' claims that the Kanza Indians spoke their name with a "z" sound. Journalists around the country liked the idea of *Kanzas* because it avoided confu-

sion with *Arkansas*. By 1859, the federal spelling had prevailed, but by then no matter how *Kansas* was pronounced, the very name spelled trouble.

Communities, even families, were divided on the issue of slavery and whether Kansas should be admitted to the Union as a Free State. Because Congress tried to evade a decision by giving Kansas the right to vote on the matter once the population reached 60,000, gangs of Missouri slaveholders tried to slow settlement by stopping westward-bound immigrants with questions about their beliefs. Would-be settlers with abolitionist views frequently were sent packing back to St. Louis. Missourians staked fake "claims" in the Kansas Territory so they could vote, and a number of territorial Kansas' first legislators were actually Missouri residents.

In some cases, there was no pretense. When abolition was the issue, Missourians voted by force, with firearms to back up claims to eligibility. As the polls closed in eastern Kansas towns, wagon drivers could be heard shouting, "All aboard for Westport" and other Missouri destinations. When abolition was put on the ballot, 628 votes were counted in the Oxford Township (now about 97th and State Line), a community of 42 residents.

Missourians increasingly meddled in Kansans' affairs and open hostility erupted. Along the border of the two states, an undeclared Civil War effectively started in the 1850s and lasted until after the surrender by General Robert E. Lee. Those years of strife earned the new territory the name "Bleeding Kansas" and brought to a standstill the commercial, agricultural, industrial and social life of Kansas City and other western Missouri towns. It began with guerrilla skirmishes and ended with outlaw bands (such as the Jesse James and Cole Younger gangs) carrying one side or another's flag as a cover for robbery, murder and destruction. In the years between, the formal war polarized communities and ravaged the land.

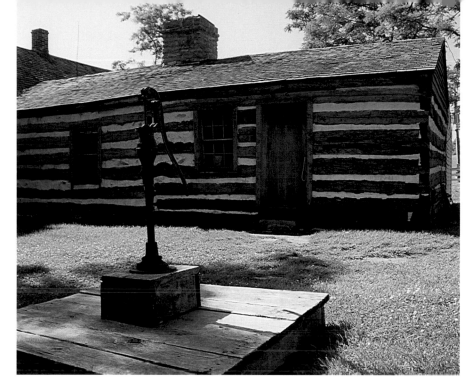

The house where outlaw Jesse James was raised (above) is now a museum in Kearney, Missouri. A bank in nearby Liberty, Missouri, also commemorates Jesse James' deeds. Now a museum, it was the site of the world's first successful peacetime, daylight bank robbery, believed to be the first official outlaw act of the notorious James Gang.

Tortuous terrain made public transit a nerve-wracking combination of convenience and thrills. Cables could snap or cars jump the track at any moment. As a result, the Kansas City Cable Company stationed a man at "the Junction," where the 9th Street hill, Main and Delaware then converged. His job was to shout "Wide Awake!" "Wide Awake!" at pedestrians in the cable car's path. Michael Tuite, an Irishman who held the job, (right in picture above) came to be simply called "Wide Awake."

People who commuted to work in the West Bottoms wholesale district, had to face a hair-raising ride on the Ninth Street Incline, built in 1885. To get to Union Depot (tall building left in picture above) passengers hurtled from the crest of Quality Hill down to the platform on Union. Some people liked the excitement enough to ride the cable car as if it were a rollercoaster for thrills on a Sunday afternoon. Electric streetcars (right) were introduced later; they proved more popular than cable and lasted as a primary form of public transit until 1957.

Tents such as this one, part of a local Civil War reenactment, appear in photographs well into the 1880s, sheltering newcomers to the area. So many hundreds of people came to Kansas City in the 1880s that there were neither jobs nor social services to support them. Many who arrived in the warm weather tried living in tent villages, not reckoning how cold winter could be at the edge of the prairie.

Until the war officially began, however, Kansas City prospered, largely from the commerce created by westward travelers. The river had floated away Independence's commercial opportunities, and border hostilities had gutted Westport's trade. Town leaders, even McCoy himself, moved to the developing city on the bluffs where business was better.

By 1860 seven railroad companies had been organized and two rail lines had promised to put a western terminus in Kansas City. Kersey Coates had poured the foundation for a grand new hotel with room in the basement for a swimming pool. More than 22,000 people lived in Jackson County.

Times looked good, but the optimism was short-lived. The Overland Stage Company declared bankruptcy in 1861, a victim of bad management, the telegraph and the railroad. Then, in 1863, bushwhackers (Union sympathizers) led by William Quantrill attacked Lawrence, Kansas, to retaliate for raids by Jayhawkers (abolitionist Kansans), and the war gained new intensity.

The culmination of the Civil War in the region came in 1864 at a battle known as the "Gettysburg of the West." The fierce battle raged across Westport and what is now Loose Park and west, into Mission Hills, Kansas. Confederate General Sterling Price and his troops were routed and fled into Arkansas. It was the last major battle of the war west of the Mississippi and was such a scarring experience that for years afterwards people said the region had four seasons: "spring, summer, Price's raid and winter."

Business in Kansas City was paralyzed. Farms were in ruins. The population was halved to 3,000. The city's upriver rival, Leavenworth, Kansas, had grown to 15,000 people and seemed likely to win the go-ahead from Congress to build a railroad bridge over the Missouri, thereby assuring that city's fortunes.

Still, Kansas Citians had seen floods, tornadoes, cholera, grasshoppers — forces of nature vast and inexplicable — as they tried to carve a town from rock and mud. War and its devastation couldn't make them quit. As before, they saw work as the saving grace. Robert Van Horn exhorted his colleagues, "Fortune never smiled on an indolent city."

So they went to work. Convinced that transportation was the key, city boosters and determined capitalists joined forces and turned their full attention to courting the railroads. By 1865 there was a short line to Lawrence, Kansas. Then the Missouri Pacific line was completed from St. Louis to Kansas City. It opened the way to the East and soon thousands of citizens looking for a place to start over after the war were disembarking on the platform marked "City of Kansas."

Towns of every size were wild to have the railroads come through. Small towns bid for the rail spur lines, promising bond issues and whatever else was necessary. Little depots soon peppered the countryside around Kansas City, but without a bridge across the Missouri, the all-important connection of East and West would go to another region and the new lines would wither away.

It was clear that two things were needed: a heavy financial commitment from the Hannibal and St. Joseph Railroad, whose bridge would span the Missouri, and Congressional approval for a bridge site. Kansas City leaders went to work on the Boston businessmen who owned the railroad. Some of the Bostonians had acquired substantial land in Kansas City and hoped to see the town grow. Meanwhile, Robert Van Horn had been elected to the U.S. House of Representatives. Once there, he slipped a bill for a bridge past the Kansas delegates, and the railroad was won for Kansas City.

Actually, a third obstacle existed: the capricious river. Few people really believed a lasting bridge could be built. The treacherous Missouri had stymied all previous attempts. However, by 1869, a new bridge, designed by engineer — and, some said, miracle worker — Octave Chanute, successfully spanned the turbulent and unpredictable "Mighty Mo."

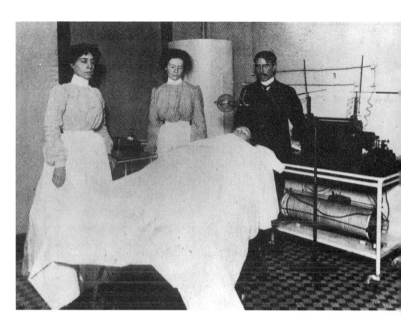

The Shawnee Indian Mission was operated by Rev. Thomas Johnson from 1839 to 1862 as a Methodist mission and school for the children of the Shawnee. The buildings, used during the Civil War as barracks, have been restored and are now open to the public as a museum.

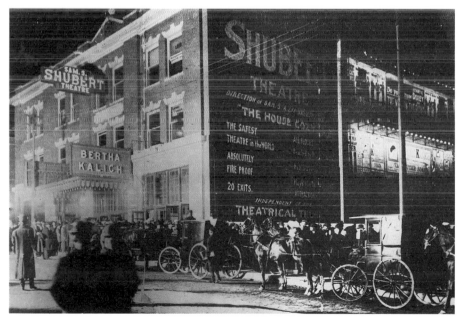

Legitimate theater has been one of Kansas City's favorite entertainments since the opening of Coates Opera House in 1870. The Gillis Theater, the Willis Wood, and the Warder Grand Theater brought stage greats such as Sarah Bernhardt, Lionel and Ethel Barrymore and George M. Cohan to town. The Shubert Theatre (above) at 10th and Baltimore (built in 1906 primarily of concrete to be fire-safe) lasted until 1935, longer than the rest. But live theater couldn't compete with the wonder of moving pictures. The Royal Theater, first of the opulent movie palaces, opened in 1914. By 1921, 55 movie theaters in the city enabled movie-goers to see an average of two shows a week.

Legendary Loula Long Combs (above, about 1908), daughter of lumber baron Robert A. Long, belonged to Kansas City's late-Victorian society which mimicked East Coast models in lifestyle and attitudes. But Loula Long transcended these conventions after a girlhood at Corinthian Hall (now the Kansas City Museum), and spent her adult life at Longview Farm where she raised championship horses. Locally known as the "Queen of the American Royal" for her interest in the yearly event, she gained a national reputation as the foremost horsewoman of her day.

Kansas City's earliest privately established hospitals were St. Joseph Hospital (1874); All Saints' Hospital, the predecessor of St. Luke's Hospital (1882); German Hospital, which became Research Medical Center (1886); Children's Mercy Hospital (1897); and Swedish Hospital, later Trinity Lutheran (1906). St. Joseph (today St. Joseph Health Center) developed the first x-ray services west of the Mississippi. The first radiology department was known as Dr. Scott's room (above, about 1910). The staff worked unshielded and many early radiologists, including Dr. Scott, died of overexposure to x-rays.

Rugged terrain and free-flowing streams challenged development efforts well into the twentieth century, but people built anyway. In 1910, OK Creek ran through what is now Penn Valley Park and at about 22nd and Wyandotte this house sat precariously close by. George Kessler was delighted by the area's many springs and streams because they gave a lively feel to the landscape. J. C. Nichols later expressed the same sentiment when he began his residential development.

The crowd's jubilation on Hannibal Bridge Dedication Day was well deserved. The bridge was a path to unparalleled growth for the city, an era in some ways a truly "golden age." By 1872 seven railways had made Kansas City a transportation hub. New people, new business, new life had come, and Kansas City had risen once again from virtual destruction.

Curiously, the same war that laid waste to so much of Kansas City's economy was about to provide an unexpected opportunity. The cattle market had come to a halt during the war and afterwards the Southwest was crowded with unsold cattle. To get rid of them, stockmen began to drive their herds to market, trying to reach rail junctures before many of the beasts died from rampant tick fever.

Kansas City became the logical collection point for transshipment to Chicago. It was an ideal arrangement. The ranchers had a selling point near the ranges. The buyers could see the cattle in a relatively civilized location and go back to plush hotels at night. Investors created a Kansas City Stock Yards Company. Farmers and cowboys began to push their animals up the trail to Abilene, Kansas, where they were loaded on rail cars headed for stockyards in the West Bottoms in Kansas City. In 1871 the first packing plant, Plankington and Armour, came to town and was soon followed by others. The hospitality business in Kansas City boomed, fueled by cowboys on the one hand and beef barons on the other.

Beef was the city's first million-dollar industry. In 1870 Kansas City banks had $3 million dollars in cattle money. The stench of the stockyards and related industries, such as soap and glue factories, permeated the Bottoms and hovered above the city by 1900. But as one old stockman later recalled, "Some people complained, but nobody who knew about business. They knew it was the smell of money."

In the newly prosperous city, the flow of cattle cash spread its gilt over surfaces and manners until they glittered. Cowboys swapped stories about the "Queen of the Cowtowns," as the city was known then, about visits to the gambling houses with their mahogany and walnut bars, gleaming brass, French glass, velvet, mirrors, saloons with no "last call" and gaming tables where the dealing never stopped. Society matrons imported furniture for lavish homes where they hosted balls and musicales.

Between 1870 and 1880 the population growth rate of Kansas City was 70 percent, double the nation's and more than six times that of cross-state rival St. Louis. During this decade the city was the largest between St. Louis and San Francisco. It gained an opera house, Exposition Hall, a new Union Depot (the third-largest train station in the world when it was built in 1878), a library, horse-drawn streetcars, a building code, a public waterworks system with 15 miles of water mains, street lamps and a two-man fire department.

An emerging middle class built substantial homes in neighborhoods chosen purely for location and price, not for their proximity to other people of similar heritage or beliefs. A generation of the recently rich was created by rocketing land prices and newfangled ways of making money, such as trading in agricultural commodities. Distinct economic classes divided the city far more than ethnic heritage did in the early years of the city's making.

On the whole, the economy flourished. Many individuals grew enormously wealthy through a variety of enterprises, including grain, beef, lumber, transportation, distribution, manufacturing, agriculture, construction, banking and professional services. A real estate boom climaxed with sales and property transfers of more than $190 million in 1887.

Paradoxically, it also was a time of great trial as the city began to face social problems without an infrastructure of social services to meet the needs. Tens of thousands of people came to the city in the 1880s as Kansas City became a transportation hub and the beef and bread capital of the nation. Immigrants stepped off the trains by the hundreds each

The enormous impact of the Civil War on the Kansas City region is not forgotten. A number of groups with authentic costumes and equipment reenact events of the period partly as living history demonstrations — and partly for the fun of it.

Armourdale merged with Kansas City, Kansas, in 1886 to become one city, and the commercial center began to edge west to 6th and Minnesota (above about 1894). New buildings and streetcar lines drew people in from surrounding residential areas.

Some of the region's most forceful leadership was provided through the editorial pages of the community's newspapers. Three early papers were working examples of Mark Twain's advice not to quarrel with a man who buys ink by the barrel.

William Rockhill Nelson (right) may well have had more effect on daily life in this region than any other individual. He arrived in 1880 and built his paper, the Evening Star, into a powerful voice. Through it he spoke out on everything, from politics to parks, crime to personal hygiene (public bath houses were part of the early parks). It has been said that Nelson never walked away from a fight, especially if it was for the common good. Called "The Baron of Brush Creek" by critics and admirers both, he left a legacy of development and pride in many areas: art, architecture, journalism, real estate, parks and public places and civic responsibility.

Robert T. Van Horn (center) came to Kansas City, Missouri in 1855 and became the city's leading strategist, spokesman and booster. He used his paper, The Journal of Commerce, to report the kind of "news" that would attract residents and investors. At different times, Van Horn served the city as postmaster, mayor, congressman, senator and even tax collector.

Louis Hammerslough, (far right) Kansas City's third permanent Jewish resident, came to town shortly before the Civil War, made a fortune in retail clothing and speculated in real estate and railroads. In 1889 he bought a German-language newspaper, renamed it the Globe, and began to compete with Van Horn and Nelson. In his paper, Hammerslough opposed the parks and boulevards system initially, but became a convert to the proposals and was named to the first park board.

Turn-of-the-century fire departments across the nation used time-saving devices invented by Fire Chief George C. Hale for his Kansas City firefighters. Hale's force was trained and drilled to such precision that spectators lined up to watch when the teams practiced at the main station on Walnut between 8th and 9th. In 1893 eight of his men and a team of matched white Arabian horses won top honors at the International Congress of Firefighters in London. Hale's methods and equipment so impressed the 10,000 firefighters gathered there that his techniques were soon copied throughout Europe.

day. But busy as the city was, there weren't enough jobs to meet the demand or enough housing to shelter everyone. Families crowded tenements that had once been fashionable apartments or they lived in makeshift housing wherever they could find open space.

The bubble burst in 1888. Kansas City's real estate boom collapsed, taking with it the hopes of many ordinary Kansas Citians who had scraped together the money for land or were buying it on monthly installments. Paper fortunes were lost overnight by people who had gambled that land prices would continue to escalate.

Land values did not come back for nearly 20 years. But many people simply hung on to what they had bought. The fact that a considerable amount of devalued land was not dumped on the market kept the shift from boom to bust from being the headlong plunge it was in other cities. Kansas City investors were tenacious, and already the area economy was sufficiently diversified to shore up the city's sagging fortunes through this period.

Even the weight of real estate reversals did not hold the city down long. It was rolling, with its progress monitored and its hopes articulated by William Rockhill Nelson, serving as the voice of his paper, the *Kansas City Star*. Nelson came to Kansas City in 1880 and began publishing the *Evening Star* (quickly nicknamed the "Twilight Twinkler" by its readers).

He championed good streets, more sidewalks, sewers, handsome public buildings, more fire protection and a bigger police force. It wasn't a popular stance in the beginning because business people saw land as a short-term investment. Large property owners weren't interested in taxes for city improvements, which were enormously costly because of the hills. Such opposition, coupled with the fact that, while other papers sold for a nickel, Nelson sold his for two cents to reach more readers, nearly bankrupted the publisher. But civic leader Kersey Coates agreed with Nelson and loaned him $5,000 at a critical time.

Then Nelson's paper and his ideas began to take hold in the community. By the end of the decade, his newspaper had the broadest readership of any paper in the city and responsible citizens began to count on his leadership. As it expanded in population, commerce, land area and, inevitably, the problems that come with growth, Kansas City had what a developing city really needed at that time: an advocate with a forum.

In the 1880s Kansas Citians either read the newspaper to know what was going on or they went to see it themselves. In 1881 when the switch was thrown on the first electric lights in Kansas City at G. Y. Smith's dry goods store, the crowd itself was described in the news: "almost every inch of available space in street, sidewalk and every gutter was covered by a jostling, crowding, pushing, hurrying mass of people."

The next year the Kawsmouth Electric Light Company provided arc lighting to businesses, and in 1885 an explosion at the gas works increased the interest of the general population in electrification. By 1886 the Edison Electric Light and Power Company made incandescent bulbs available to private homes.

A telephone exchange was initiated in 1879 with 30 subscribers. By 1882 a single sheet listing 58 names was the telephone "book" issued by the Missouri and Kansas Telephone Company. Necessity encouraged this invention, as the city was stretching its boundaries. In 1885 the city limits moved south to 31st and east to Cleveland Avenue.

The wealthy residents of Quality Hill and Knob Hill began to tire of the smell of the stockyards wafting up from the Bottoms and to feel hemmed in by the increasing numbers of immigrants and the poor living downtown. Those who could afford it started to move: blacks to the neighborhoods east of Troost and south of 13th, whites to the south and west.

The commercial district between Ninth Street and the levee, mostly along Main, Delaware and Grand, was finally nearly level

Farmer John B. Wornall built an imposing brick Greek Revival home in 1858 in the center of his 500-acre farm, which was located south of Westport along the Santa Fe Trail. The house was used as a hospital during the Civil War. Today, as a museum at 61st Terrace and the road named for Wornall, the house reveals the lifestyle of prosperous mid-19th century Missouri farmers.

Early health care was home-based; hospitals were considered places for the indigent who could not afford private nursing. The first local private hospitals, usually converted dwellings, were founded by physicians or religious and ethnic groups. Kansas City had a 15-bed public hospital in 1871. General Hospital (above) was built in 1903; General Hospital No. 2 was built in 1928 to serve the black population. By 1959, the General Hospitals were combined to eliminate racial segregation, and during the next decade, a health complex on Hospital Hill brought together Truman Medical Center (which replaced the old General Hospital), Children's Mercy Hospital and the new University of Missouri-Kansas City Medical School.

In 1903 President Teddy Roosevelt visited Kansas City, and crowds thronged to see his carriage drive down The Paseo (above). The President reportedly couldn't stop exclaiming about the beauty, variety and number of trees in the city.

Entrepreneurs came from farms and small towns to seek opportunity in Kansas City in the early years of the twentieth century. The YMCA at 11th and Oak housed many aspiring young businessmen, including Joyce C. Hall who started a post card business there. In 1910 he moved his business to the Braley Building at 308 East 10th, taking a small room on the third floor above the shoe shine shop.

No doubt pleased to be away from public transportation for a day, Metropolitan Street Railway employees enjoyed a company outing in 1910 with automobiles and motorcycles.

and beginning to bustle. It no longer made a gracious residential neighborhood. Soon new mansions were going up in the Northeast along Independence Boulevard and to the south, following fashionable Troost, or farther south to the exclusive enclave of Hyde Park.

Moreover, horse-drawn trolleys and an ambitious cable railway system created ready transportation throughout the area. The more reclusive well-to-do could live on virtual estates far from the center city and be assured that servants and services could reach them. Middle-class families could move to the developing suburbs and use public transportation to reach work, shopping and leisure activities.

The migrations were largely unplanned, and homes and commercial buildings were mixed with abandon. By the 1890s Kansas City was sprawling and becoming steadily less attractive.

In earlier decades, the simple abundance of green trees and natural beauty had offered forgiving relief from the muddy streets and hodgepodge building. But near the end of the century, the cleared land left unobstructed views — and they were not pretty. Abandoned streetcar lines and half-built suburbs were testaments to the real estate losses of the late 1880s. Too many newcomers and too few jobs spawned shantytowns that housed the poor within sight of fine homes and major thoroughfares. Clearly another kind of disaster was overtaking the city, less immediate than tornadoes or floods, but perhaps more damaging.

Kansas City began moving toward a solution under the aegis of the Commercial Club of Kansas City. Made up of nearly 60 prominent businessmen, the club was the nucleus of civic leadership and a forerunner of today's Chamber of Commerce. The group formed in 1887 to promote trade and industrial development. But their meetings always turned to topics of broader citizenship. They took as their slogan, "Make Kansas City a good place to live," and threw their support behind projects designed to clean up crime

and filth in the city; to emphasize and preserve its natural attributes with parks and planned building; to support cultural activities; to increase amusement and leisure opportunities; and, of course, to develop the city's economic base and commercial success.

Whatever struggles were required to "civilize" the city, its economy was strong as the century ended. Kansas City had one of the largest cattle and grain markets in the world. Annual receipts at the stockyards alone were more than $125 million. The city had 14 grain elevators and a Board of Trade to handle the millions of bushels of grain shipped through the city yearly. The Kansas City Smelting and Refining Company in the Argentine District of Kansas City, Kansas, was called the "largest and most completely equipped metallurgical works in the world."

There was a new city hall and, at 5th and Oak, a new Jackson County courthouse, both completed in 1892. A new convention hall was finished in 1899. There were 12 miles of boulevards and more under construction, and 1,691 acres of parks. When the century ended, 164,745 residents were counted by the Census in Kansas City, Missouri, and in Kansas City, Kansas, 51,418.

But the high hopes welcoming the new century were soon dashed. In 1903 the Missouri River flooded the Bottoms, home to thousands of poor families and immigrants and the manufacturing and wholesaling heart of the region. The flood swept away the stockyards and filled up the Union Depot, destroyed the bridges and submerged utility plants. The city was without gas, electricity, drinking water, telephone service, rail transportation or fire protection. The population faced the potential of epidemic disease.

Again, the city rose, its spirit unbroken. The public sector kept order and soon restored essential services. The private sector — volunteers from businesses, churches and synagogues, social and professional clubs — took on the relief effort of feeding, sheltering and clothing refugees. So much relief money

Alexander Majors built this house in 1856 at what is now 82nd and State Line Road. Its 43 windows were an almost unimaginable luxury; glass had to be transported upriver to Kansas City at great expense. Majors, founder of the Overland State Company and a partner in the short-lived Pony Express, was a rarity in the tough bull-whacking business — a courtly, religious man who opposed drinking and gambling. His workers had to sign an oath: "While I am in the employ of A. Majors I agree not to use profane language, not to get drunk, not to gamble, not to treat animals cruelly, and not to do anything else that is not compatible with the conduct of a gentleman." On the National Register of Historical Places, the house site today includes a rebuilt barn, blacksmith and wagon-making shops and a Conestoga wagon display.

The first horseless carriage in Kansas City was owned by John Higdon, who never drove it in daylight because it frightened horses. In 1901, the city's first auto accident occurred at 11th and Locust when two steam Locomobiles collided. By 1908 an auto show in the Convention Hall (above) showed the latest models available at the city's 22 dealerships.

Before World War I, the Kansas City garment industry was reasonably successful manufacturing work clothes. During the war, workers such as these shown in 1917 began to use an assembly line method, each stitching different sections of a finished piece. This method had been used for men's clothing but Kansas City garment workers were the first to apply it to women's wear. Within a decade, local companies produced much of the ready-to-wear women's clothing in America.

A permissible social activity for young people at the turn of the century was meeting for a sarsaparilla or phosphate at a corner drug store like Clark's Pharmacy at 63rd and Raytown Road (today the site of a United Missouri Bank). By 1915 (above) an outdoor porch for dancing had been added to the store along with a sign of the times: Drive In.

was raised so quickly in Kansas City, Missouri, that funds donated from outside the city limits were turned over to Kansas City, Kansas. The area began to dig out and rebuild within days.

The next year another, smaller flood derailed much of the reconstruction work and stimulated a movement that eventually resulted in a Union Station and railroad hub located on higher ground and an Intercity Viaduct elevated across the Bottoms to keep the two largest Kansas City centers of commerce connected.

Despite the floods, business was good. Before the decade ended, a Standard Oil refinery brought jobs and people to Sugar Creek in Jackson County and more than 30 manufacturing concerns began operating in the Blue Valley area. The downtown skyline was up to 15 stories with the Commerce Building; the public City Hospital was built; and Swope Park had a zoo. Across the Missouri River a levee built in 1909 made it possible for North Kansas City to establish a community relatively safe from floods, and a new bridge, the Armour-Swift-Burlington, supported more cross-river traffic.

In 1910 it was clear Kansas City was no longer merely the "City of the Future," as it had been called for 60 years. The future, it seemed, had arrived. Puffing chimneys sent up smoke signals of industrial success. So many incidents of automobiles at odds with carriages occurred that newspapers tired of reporting them. Businesses and many homes had electric lights. Ready-to-wear shops attracted customers away from the best dressmakers. Social problems had outgrown the safety net of private caring, so Kansas City organized the first full public department of welfare in the United States.

Government itself was changing. In Kansas City, it had evolved from small town meetings to forms intended to lead an increasingly sophisticated city. Kansas City was governed in 1890 by a city council with an upper house elected at large and a lower house elected by ward.

Wards dominated political parties, however, and ward chieftains took care of their own. Until James Pendergast, there was really no local centralized government and little order to the party process. A saloonkeeper, Pendergast earned a devoted following among laborers who frequented his establishment. Elected alderman in 1892, he gained the support of other ward chieftains, and by the turn of the century he was the North End's political leader.

When Jim Pendergast's candidate, James Reed, was elected mayor in 1900, a powerful patronage position went to Jim's brother, Tom. When Jim died in 1911, Tom took over his council seat and began to organize other areas of the city. Soon he had enough control that his gambling, prostitution and saloon enterprises were safe — at least from the police.

Citizens' groups weren't keen on protection for such activities. In fact, as early as the 1890s, some citizen groups had wanted to "clean up" Kansas City by ridding the town of gambling and crime and by creating a less corrupt form of government. In 1905 a revamped city charter expanded the mayor's powers of appointment, both for city officials and various city agencies. Ironically, this "reform" made a political boss' power even stronger, as long as his mayoral candidates won.

About the time the country entered World War I, reformers again tried and failed to change the city government, this time to a council-city manager structure. Not until several years after the Great War did the issue of restructuring the city government rise again, and by then "Boss" Tom Pendergast was reaching the height of his power.

In 1920 the corner of 12th and Walnut (above, looking west) was a busy commercial area with Frank Wachter's popular buffet, one of the nation's first cafeterias, and the Regent, one of the city's many movie theaters.

The Mahaffie Farmstead and Stagecoach Stop (1100 Kansas City Road) in Olathe, Kansas, was built in 1865. It was the farm home of J.B. Mahaffie, who came to the area in 1857 and soon became Olathe's largest landowner. Between 1865 and 1869 the home served as a stagecoach stop on the road to Lawrence and Fort Scott, Kansas, and to Santa Fe, New Mexico.

What was then the biggest crowd in Kansas City history turned out for the Armistice Day parade in 1919. Every branch of service was represented, along with nurses and other groups. It signaled in some ways the end of the city's early period. The war encouraged people to think globally and to see Kansas City's potential in a new light.

The 1914 opening of the new Union Station gave Kansas City a grand building in keeping with the self-image the thriving city had developed. It also effectively moved the rail terminal away from any threat of inundation by one of the Missouri's periodic floods.

Frank Pisciotta's ice wagon (above, about 1926) was a familiar sight in the 1920s, along with other horse- and mule-drawn delivery vehicles. Later, Pisciotta began a fruit and vegetable business, still in operation.

Anyone looking north from 27th and Main in 1927 (above) would have had difficulty foreseeing the area's development potential. The Liberty Memorial Mall area had not yet been fully developed and was still a rough limestone outcropping with the roof of the Union Station just visible beyond it. Across Main, "Signboard Hill" (with the landmark Western Auto building in the right center of the photo) could hardly have been imagined as a future home for Crown Center.

Fresh air and organized outdoor activities were considered important to personal health and civic welfare in the early twentieth century. Formal recreation programs became an important part of community life through sports and games in public parks and at private clubs. The region's challenging topography encouraged regular hiking forays, including this one in about 1915. Led by J. C. Nichols (second from right in photo above), the group is crossing a ford on Brush Creek at what is now Mission Hills Country Club.

Union Cemetery (far right) was established in 1843 and so named because it formed a "union" between Westport and the new Town of Kansas. Many famous Kansas Citians are buried there.

Inspired by George Kessler's work on the local parks system and by the tradition of European landscaping that combined art with public space, J.C. Nichols began to buy pieces of art to beautify his residential developments. In 1925 eight columns were brought from Verona, Italy, to create a park with a stone terrace and two pools (right, in 1925) at the intersection of Mission Drive, Ensley Lane and Overhill Road.

The Urban Frontier

Air traffic was outgrowing the Fairfax Airport in Kansas City, Kansas, when Municipal Airport was built across the river in 1927. It rapidly became one of the busiest airports in the world. Flying had captured America's imagination: crowds turned out to welcome Charles Lindburgh to Municipal's dedication and avidly followed the air adventures of Kansan Amelia Earhart. Kansas City had some notable aviatrixes including Betty Browning and Harriett Barrett (above, with their Inland Sport aircraft at Fairfax in 1932).

(right) Magnificent Longview Farm in Lee's Summit, Missouri, was built in 1914 as the country estate of Robert A. Long. It was regarded by many as the world's most beautiful farm. The farm was completely self-sufficient with its own water and telephone systems; steam heat in all the buildings; electricity throughout the property; homes for the farm's nearly 200 employees; stables and cattle barns; flower and vegetable gardens, pastures and orchards. Today the restored 21,000-foot mansion, the show-horse stable with its original Tiffany chandeliers, and other Longview buildings are used for functions from weddings to conventions.

After World War I, Kansas City's economy continued building on its strengths — agribusiness, manufacturing and distribution — but it was clear that change was in the wind. The natural advantages of its rivers and rail hubs were no longer sufficient to guarantee the area market superiority. More sophisticated networks of communications and transportation were available, and smaller towns and cities no longer had to depend on Kansas City as a jumping-off place.

Citizens were more sophisticated, too, or at least less naive. They had experienced "global thinking" during the war years. Now their opinions on everything from skirt lengths to government were shaped by forces far from their neighborhoods.

Across the country, habits of mind and mores changed; some said fundamental moral standards changed, too. Handshake business deals were largely forgotten as contracts and complex regulations became the norm. A pell-mell opportunism intoxicated a nation already high on victory. Americans rushed headlong into business, politics and pleasure.

These forces affected Kansas City, of course, and made the 1920s an unforgettable decade. Still, the nation's best values have historically been held close to its geographic heart, and that wasn't changed much by the Roaring Twenties. While Kansas City boasted some of the hottest nightclubs in the country, the neighborliness and caring that had been such a part of the frontier years still remained. Important social services and philanthropic agencies were established; the parks and boulevards system continued to grow; health

care and education took on new dimensions. And Kansas City became a leader in home ownership, with a greater percentage of families in houses of their own than in any city in the nation.

While the nation remembers the 1920s nostalgically as a wild party before the storm of the Depression, for Kansas City the decade was more complex than that.

In 1925 pressures for reform led to a new city charter, establishing a city manager form of government. The idea passed with Boss Tom Pendergast's support: the new charter meant far fewer council positions to influence as he took control of the city from top to bottom. A Missouri Supreme Court decision established home rule for police about the same time, giving Pendergast still more latitude to operate.

The Pendergast machine's power escalated (along with that of the Democratic Party in Kansas City and Jackson County), reaching its zenith between 1925 and 1939. Kansas City's reputation then as a "sin city" was well-deserved. Hundreds of clubs operated around the clock. Liquor, prostitution and gambling concerns routinely bought police protection. Criminals unlucky enough to be arrested went free — if they had the right connections. The city was wide open, as evidenced by Boss Tom's racetrack north of the Missouri River, which was built in flagrant disregard for Missouri's anti-gambling laws. The track featured signs over the betting windows that read "donations" and "refunds."

There's no doubt that crime was high during the period, but opinions about the rest of Pendergast's "accomplishments" have become steadily more divided over time. Some still hold him in contempt for ignoring

The Great Depression couldn't keep a lid on Kansas City night life, which turned the 1930s into a decade-long dance party. Couples out on the town could choose among 50 jazz clubs between 12th and 18th, or head for a more sedate evening at the Pla-Mor ballroom at 3142 Main (above, about 1930) where the dance floor was buoyed by 7,000 felt cushions. Opened in 1927, the Pla-Mor was the largest amusement complex in the country with an ice rink and, after 1931, the largest fresh-water swimming pool west of the Mississippi. The population shift to the suburbs after the war caused the ballroom to close in 1951.

the city's best interests. Others revere his mercies to the poor in his wards. Some view the years of "Tom's Town" as a tragic period of unfair distribution of business opportunity and rewards. Others say that the worst of the Depression was avoided in Kansas City because the Pendergast machine employed people and attracted federal funds to the city during those difficult years.

Whatever the verdict of history regarding Tom Pendergast, it's clear that the Kansas City region managed not only to endure but to prevail during the twenty checkered years between the World Wars. People worked hard, as they always have in Kansas City. Work weeks were commonly seven days with a day off every two weeks. Double shifts produced 16-hour days for many industries, and laborers, shop clerks, soda jerks and others in the "service" sector regularly worked 11- to 16-hour days.

The greater metropolis began to develop in earnest, with energy and people spreading out from the confluence of the rivers, carrying along the work ethic and sense of style that had created a real city from a rock ledge in only 80 years.

In two obvious ways, the area was really moving: cars and planes. Automobiles and aviation revamped transportation in the region as they did in the nation.

Nothing could top the growth of the local aviation industry. One day in 1919, a seven-minute flight from Raytown to Kansas City allowed a hay press salesman to get emergency replacement parts to a customer in the field. With that kind of service, the future of local commercial aviation was assured. Shortly after Municipal Airport was dedicated across the river from downtown Kansas City in 1927, it attracted regional and national air carriers and quickly became one of the busiest airports in the country.

Kansas City soon was one of the world's leading manufacturers of automobiles and auto parts as well. In addition to the economic boost this gave the city, the auto changed the

region in other ways. Automobiles were adapted into trucks and used to transport the kinds of goods that might formerly have gone by river. Autos also promoted suburban growth within the region. Cars helped drive the city's steady expansion southward through annexations — Westport in 1897, Waldo (to about 71st) in 1909.

Modern zoning practices were unknown then, creating situations like the one in which industry threatened desirable land tracts close to where the Plaza is today. Seeing the huge land holdings to the south and west that were still owned by families such as the Wards, Wornalls and Armours, it was easy for young real estate developer J.C. Nichols to imagine residential environments there, completely controlled and protected from undesirable forces of industrial growth.

When the Republican National Convention met here in 1928 to nominate Herbert Hoover, *A Hotel Greeter's Guide to Kansas City* was able to offer a litany of achievements. These included a regional population of more than half a million people; a streetcar system with 305 miles of track; 71 national and state banks; the largest Livestock Exchange Building in the world; a Fine Arts Institute and a Conservatory of Music; various colleges and a medical school; 400 houses of worship; a $15 million fund to begin building a world-class art museum; and many other wonders.

But the stock market crashed a year later, and Kansas City, along with the rest of the nation, plummeted into the Great Depression.

Why Kansas City survived the Depression as well as it did is the subject of debate. The unemployment rate was substantially lower here than it was nationally, and the mixed economic base kept disaster at bay. Kansas Citians took their usual hope-for-the-best attitude to the polls in 1931 and passed a $40 million bond issue that authorized the construction during the next decade of a new city hall, police building, Municipal Auditorium, courthouse and miles of concrete roads. Public works projects altered the

Implements in the Agricultural Hall of Fame at Bonner Springs, Kansas, recall the "sod bustin'" days of the region as well as its rich agricultural heritage and promise. The National Farmers' Memorial is located at the Hall of Fame.

Begun as a show of purebred cattle in 1899, the American Royal gained its name in 1901, added horse shows in 1903 and acquired its own buildings in 1922. By 1935 (above) the American Royal had become what it remains today: one of the premier livestock shows in the world.

By 1932 nearly 80,000 cars were registered locally and intersection lights had become a necessity. The one at Linwood Boulevard and The Paseo is still there today, like a monument to an era of more stately traffic control.

The Kansas City region survived the Depression in better shape than many cities in large measure because of significant assistance through the Works Progress Administration. By 1939 over 100 federal offices were located in Kansas City to supervise many "New Deal" agencies. Local WPA programs, such as public canning kitchens (above) and construction programs, helped individual workers and families. Some of Kansas City's finest building projects (including municipal buildings and park improvements) occurred during this period.

The Country Club Plaza, the nation's first shopping district created with automobile traffic in mind, was planned in 1922 by architect Edward Buehler Delk for the J.C. Nichols Company. By the late 1930s (above), Nichols' dream of a Spanish-style shopping plaza was in place. The Chandler Building with its landmark smokestack at 47th and Mill Creek Parkway (left, seen from what is now Mill Creek Park) was already there when the planning began and its curved facade was a Plaza fixture until it was razed in 1961 to make way for the Giralda Tower, Swansons, and the fountain courtyard now called Chandler Court.

city skyline and produced a number of buildings of lasting beauty.

Business tolerated Boss Tom Pendergast's influence during the early '30s, accepting kickbacks as part of doing business. But when machine-gun toting goons disrupted the 1934 elections, leaving four dead, the business community had had enough. Efforts at reform began in earnest.

The reformers might have gotten Boss Tom if horses and bad health hadn't gotten him first. Tom Pendergast had a gambling habit that squandered a million dollars a year. His efforts to support it attracted the attention of the Internal Revenue Service, and in 1939, he went to jail for income tax evasion. His organization collapsed, and the Pendergast era was over.

Tom Pendergast had been a town builder in many ways, but in others a destroyer. He virtually washed away the city budget, leaving a debt of $22 million. Again, facing a problem they believed hard work could resolve, citizens set to the task. The "Lady Reformers," a group of women who worked hard in the campaign to get rid of machine politics, made lapel pins: little brooms to represent the clean-up. For professional leadership, the city brought in L.P. Cookingham, a young city manager from Michigan, to be the "new broom that sweeps clean." With Mayor John B. Gage's support, Cookingham revised city government in Kansas City, eliminated the public debt, put the city on sound economic footing and developed a reputation for outstanding city management that endures nationally today.

One of the questions that might have faced the reformers — what to do about the city's economy during the 1940s — was answered by war. Even before the United States officially entered World War II, some of the area's leaders were in Washington, assuring the government that Kansas City could handle any defense contracts sent its way. Only one new industry had come to the city during World War I, and no business

people wanted to see that pattern repeated.

When the war contracts began to come in, they jump-started the economy of the region and quickly jolted it into high gear. Munitions factories, air-, land- and seacraft factories, chemical production, war-related research and manufacturing of all kinds combined to make Kansas City an industrial city.

Near the end of the decade, voters again passed a major bond issue, this time for $41.5 million for airport improvements and highways. This set the stage for the principal achievements of the 1950s, continued economic growth and property annexation by the city.

During the 1950s the city gained population; new post-war residential areas were built up, and commercial interests continued to succeed. As many of the war industries converted to peacetime functions, the service sector began to grow steadily, with attorneys, accountants, insurers and other professionals building firms to meet the needs of expanding businesses.

L.P. Cookingham resigned in 1959, and the city drifted without strong administrative leadership for four years, during which time 10 city managers tried their luck. In 1963 Ilus W. Davis was elected mayor and, until 1971, he served as what some called "the architect of the city's renaissance."

The 1960s were undeniably difficult. Business was stagnant in many quarters. Traditional strengths weakened. The packing industry closed down. Train traffic slowed. The garment industry declined. Suburbs sapped the vitality of the central city. Racial discord erupted, as it did in many cities throughout the country. But once it became evident that the quality of life in the city was truly in peril, individuals, citizens' groups and businesses banded together to fight back.

Relations between the public and private sector grew closer during these years as people came to understand that a modern city could only develop with team effort. Distinguished business and community leaders

The annual Auto Show at Municipal Auditorium was an event eagerly anticipated by area drivers, especially teenaged boys. The 1959 show (above) reflected the glory years of automaking nationwide. Kansas City was second only to Detroit in auto production and the auto industry represented a significant segment of the area economy.

Established in 1943 to foster regional development through science and technology, Midwest Research Institute soon gained a reputation for producing high-quality research for private industry. In the 1950s, for example, MRI scientists used flash photolysis equipment (above) to develop fire-extinguishing agents. In recent decades, MRI's focus has broadened and today it is one of the nation's preeminent research institutions with a broad range of private and public sector clients, including the U.S. Department of Energy for which MRI has operated the Solar Research Energy Institute since 1977.

Formed in 1919 the Kansas City Monarchs baseball team traveled the Midwest in the 1920s and 1930s when baseball was rigidly segregated. The Monarchs attracted awesomely talented players and thrilled their fans with feats such as 43 straight wins in 1943. A Monarchs player, Jackie Robinson, was the first black player to sign with a major league team, the Brooklyn Dodgers, in 1947. Monarch pitcher Satchel Paige (far right) eventually played for the Cleveland Indians, the St. Louis Browns and the Kansas City A's, and became a legend .

The Liberty Memorial was conceived as a monument to peace and to commemorate those who had fought and died in World War I. Designed by New York architect H. Van Buren Magonigle, the memorial was dedicated in 1926 by President Calvin Coolidge. The Museum and Archives (in the west building) is the only military museum in the United States specializing in the first world war. Two enormous sphinxes guard the entrance and symbolize Future, with eyes shielded against the unknown, and Memory, with face shrouded to forget the horror of war.

formed a Civic Council in 1965 that was dedicated to helping Kansas City realize its promise in all areas of city life. Identical in spirit to the group that met in the Coates House Hotel a hundred years before to set goals for the city, the Civic Council has worked now for more than a quarter century to help address critical issues.

The succeeding mayoral administrations — of Mayor Charles B. Wheeler during the 1970s and Richard L. Berkley in the 1980s — continued to encourage public-private partnerships that would most successfully address the economic and social issues that arise in all modern urban centers.

Population in the metropolitan area grew to about 1.5 million people by the close of the 1980s, and the city spread out. By 1984 Kansas City, Missouri, covered 316 square miles and was surrounded by thriving suburban communities and smaller cities. These smaller communities began to come into their own when, in 1956, the Eisenhower Administration secured passage of the Interstate Highway Act. In Kansas City, that legislation funded expressways throughout the area and a freeway loop around the central business district. During the following thirty years, other ambitious highway projects were built. Today the city is ringed by functional, high-speed roadways that move traffic quickly throughout the region and encourage strong regional shopping centers and residential communities.

In the early 1970s a new airport about 20 miles north of downtown Kansas City, sparked commercial and residential development to the north. A dynamic business corridor along College Boulevard in Overland Park, Kansas, stimulated growth to the south. New industries found homes in Lee's Summit, Blue Springs, Grandview, and other developing communities to the east and southeast in Missouri. The new Truman Sports Complex, built in eastern Jackson County, in 1973, also drew people in that direction. As in many other cities, the once-vital downtown area went into decline.

Taking up the challenge, businesses, investors, retailers, developers and others turned their efforts toward revitalization. A $3.5 billion urban renaissance was well under way by 1975. By the mid-1980s the city was enjoying a $5 billion construction boom, with much of the new building going on downtown. Quality Hill, Westport, the Crown Center area, the Garment District and the River Market area have moved on their own paths toward realizing a shared vision of a vital city core.

Voters have had an important say in the region's recent progress. Since 1983, $1.3 billion worth of capital improvement programs have been passed. The city's success at the polls is rated among the best — if not the very best — in the nation. Since the mid-1980s, more than 700 capital improvement projects, including 500 neighborhood projects, have improved life in the city, from building curbs to skyscrapers.

It is clear that the challenges of the twentieth century are more overwhelming than even the task of blasting a usable town site out of rock and mud. Changing social needs steadily outdistance the resources available to meet them. These trials make up an urban frontier perhaps less navigable than the vast wilderness travelers to this region confronted a hundred and fifty years ago.

Pioneers in that wide-open landscape found similarities in each other's common goals. Today, more often it is the differences in people that seem to show, as they jostle for space, necessities, rewards. Yet, anyone who lives here senses that beneath the differences — perhaps, in some ways, *because* of them — a deep connection underlies the whole. Newcomers sense it and inquire: What binds us, across so many map lines, with so many differing pasts and pursuits?

One of the uses of memory is to look back for patterns. In the history of this area, it becomes clear that people here value the same things. Fairness and integrity, perseverance and play. They believe they can make change

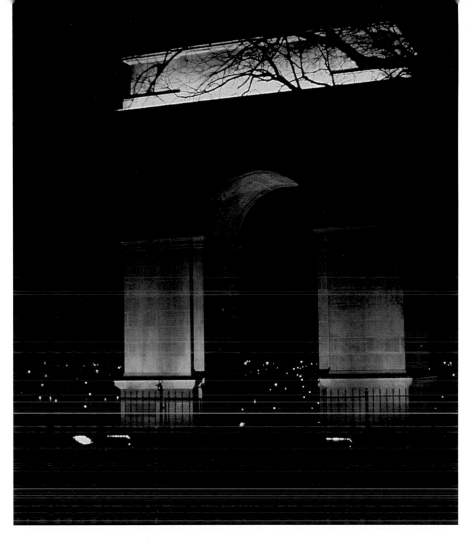

Social change marked the 1960s and 1970s in Kansas City as in other parts of the country. Demonstrations on behalf of many causes included a stop in Kansas City by Native-American participants on the Trail of Broken Treaties in March 1976. The demonstrators set up teepees in Penn Valley Park near the Pioneer Mother statue.

Kansas City has a long memory for valor and sacrifice. Memorials to the veterans of various wars can be seen throughout the region in parks and other public places. To commemorate their men lost in World War I, a memorial arch was erected in 1924 by the people of Rosedale, Kansas, (chartered in 1872 and named for the wild roses which grew there). The arch (above left), which was designed by local architect John Leroy Marshall as a scaled-down version of Paris' Arc de Triomphe de l'Etoile, was rededicated in 1964 to veterans of all wars. The Rosedale Memorial Arch is located off Rainbow Boulevard on a hill once commonly known as Mt. Marty.

The Vietnam Veterans Memorial (43rd and J.C. Nichols Parkway) receives scores of visitors, many of whom leave remembrances at the wall where the names of the dead are recorded. Dedicated in 1985, the memorial honors men and women who fought and died in Vietnam.

happen with hard work. They believe kindness and hospitality are a stranger's due. They believe life should be fun sometimes.

Maybe these are "Midwestern values." It is a phrase often used as a catchall to describe the fact that people here are decent. And as well as being decent, they are hopeful. In essentially American and true frontier fashion, this city sees itself forever grabbing the second chance, starting over to make good, becoming what was meant to be. If ever there's a hesitation in confronting problems, it is not from lack of courage, but rather reflects sufficiency of hope and the faith that things will come right after all.

And indeed, over more than a hundred and fifty years, most things have.

In 1955 TransWorld Airlines was Kansas City's hometown airline (above) and the downtown skyline was substantial.

The pull of the suburbs had almost sapped the vitality of downtown by the mid-1960s, but in 1965 (above) the traditional post-Thanksgiving crowd of holiday shoppers still thronged the streets to shop and see the decorated stores.

Old-fashioned boosterism helped trigger a revival of visitors' interest in Kansas City. In the early 1970s area business leaders devised a campaign called "Prime Time" to attract media attention and convention business to the area. It worked and 1976 was a banner year. The H. Roe Bartle Convention Center opened downtown; Kemper Arena opened nearby and the Republican National Convention (right) came to town.

(far right) More than $5 billion in commercial construction changed the face of Kansas City during the 1980s. In 1985 dreams of a revitalized downtown were becoming as real as 40-story shapes against the sky.

Enterprise

If hard work doesn't agree with you,
or you can't get on without luxuries,
stay where you are.
If you don't have pluck and perseverance;
stay where you are.

"How and Where to Get a Living:
A Sketch of the Garden of the West"
Atchison, Topeka & Santa Fe Railroad Co., 1876

Farms to Far Lands

Industriousness and craftsmanship are sources of pride in virtually every area of endeavor. Kansas Citians believe one person can still make a difference.

(opening) The College Boulevard corridor in Overland Park is one of the region's fastest-growing business communities.

(right) The old line "Goin' to Kansas City" has new meaning. With more freeway miles per capita than any other American city with more than a million residents — and still more highways under way — greater Kansas City is an easy drive. The average time commuters spend getting to work throughout the metroplex is only 25 minutes.

It's been said that Kansas City is like the proverbial boy or girl next-door — such a friend that romance seems impossible to imagine. Doing business in the region is somewhat the same with opportunities so near to hand they are easy to take for granted.

One example is location. Transportation, distribution and communications are affordable here because Kansas City is in the middle of just about everywhere: within 250 miles of both the geographic and population centers of the United States. Local businesses accept this as a given, but outsiders recognize it as a tremendous asset.

Likewise easy to overlook is the advantage of the extra-long business day. The Central time zone and still-strong frontier habits of rising early and working late make the Kansas City business day potentially one of the most productive in the nation. When New Yorkers get to work at 9 a.m., Kansas City businesspeople are at their desks, ready to go. When Californians are returning their late-afternoon calls, Kansas City switchboards are still answering.

Middle-American values are strong assets for business. People expect to work hard, work together and produce quality.

It's a region where individual initiative is prized and encouraged. Throughout the frontier period, virtually every business started as an entrepreneur's vision.

In 1857, J. F. Richards began selling hardware to westward travelers. With his salesman, John Conover, he established a hardware business, and as times changed so did Richards and Conover Steel Company.

Today it is the oldest continuously existing business in Kansas City.

In the mid-1880s, Arthur Stillwell founded the Kansas City Suburban Belt Railroad, forerunner to Kansas City Southern Industries, which today operates subsidiaries in transportation, data processing for financial services, insurance, real estate and other interests.

In 1908, W.T. Grant, a homesteader's son, had the idea that the newfangled automobiles meant businessmen would need accident insurance; he founded Business Men's Assurance Company, which became a billion-dollar, multinational corporation.

Two years later, Joyce C. Hall began selling postcards from a shoe box he kept under his bed in his room at the YMCA. The company he founded, Hallmark Cards, Inc. transformed the way people communicate with each other. Now headed by his son, Donald J. Hall, the company has grown into the industry's leader and an international corporation in its own right.

The magic kept working. In 1950, Ewing Kauffman saw the future in health care, capitalized on a stable work force and central distribution and built Marion Laboratories. Today it is the worldwide pharmaceutical giant Marion Merrell Dow, Inc.

In 1966, Paul Henson brought a small-town telephone company to Kansas City, Missouri and it grew into United Telecommunications, Inc. and US Sprint.

Being smack-dab in the middle of everything has contributed to Kansas City's ranking first nationally in foreign trade zone space; frozen food storage and distribution; greeting card publishing; hard winter wheat marketing; instrument landing systems manufacture;

Public transportation at its jolliest is provided by the trolleys operated by the Kansas City Trolley Corp. Year-round, the trolleys carry passengers between the Plaza and the River Market area with regular stops along the way.

Grain elevators in Edgerton, Kansas, are emblems of the region's century-old prominence in wheat production. Today Kansas City is the world's largest winter wheat futures market, first in the nation in marketing hard winter wheat (the country's main bread and export wheat), second in wheat flour production and third in grain elevator storage space.

and underground storage space. It ranks second only to Detroit in auto assembly and third in truck assembly and is the nation's second largest rail center and wheat flour producer.

Today the results of a hundred and fifty years of taking care of business shows in a steady economy and an ever-increasing appeal to new business. Moreover, the diverse population makes the region a kind of crystal ball for the nation. The demographic makeup mirrors the nation's in terms of age, income, education level and family size. If Kansas Citians want to buy a product or see a movie, chances are good that the rest of the country will, too.

Manageable media costs and a stable economy attract companies conducting trial runs of all kinds of products and services from diapers to wine coolers to first-run movies. Kansas City said "yes" to the first McDonald's Happy Meal, and the rest is fast-food history. The U.S. Census Bureau used the metropolitan area for its 1990 Census "dress rehearsal."

From the beginning, the success of business in the region goes back to the necessities — food and goods required to sustain life — and to the basics of understanding the customer.

The first towns along the Missouri and Kansas rivers were a combination of prosperous farms and bustling little market areas. Independence, Missouri, was the most successful center of commerce in the years between the westward movement of the 1820s and the Civil War.

Kansas City, Kansas, began as a scattering of farms, some owned by the Wyandot Indians who were resettled there from Ohio in 1843. A Town of Wyandot post office was established in 1855, and a group of Kansas City, Missouri, businessmen purchased the core of the town and platted it in 1857. Two years later, Wyandot was incorporated as a city and was the site of the convention to draw up a constitution for the state of Kansas.

The little city struggled through the war and began to grow again when the first

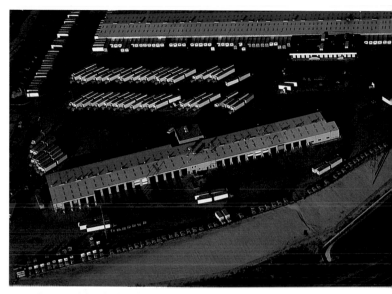

Urban and rural realities blend happily here. Regional progress still includes agriculture, always an economic mainstay in the area where six of every 10 jobs are related to agriculture.

Farm boys could make big dreams come true in Kansas City. George Powell, Sr. combined a rural education and penchant for hard work and came up with a winning formula for Yellow Freight System, Inc., now one of the nation's largest trucking concerns.

Few regional cities would consider fire part of a regular work day, but for a farmer in Johnson County, Kansas, controlled burning is important to next year's crop.

Traditional shopping values — friendly merchants and cheery sidewalks — are helping bring shoppers back to revitalized downtowns such as this one in North Kansas City.

Symbolic of the city's rebirth after the Civil War was the Coates House Hotel at 10th and Broadway. Across the street (left building, seen from rear) Kersey Coates also built an opera house which attracted some of the finest national and international entertainment of the day. Beside it in the early 1870s was a cow pasture.

packing plant was built in the Central Industrial District in 1868. From that time, it developed a solid industrial base of railroads, stockyards and ancillary industries, such as soap manufacturing. It had annexed nearby Riverview and Armstrong by 1886. Later that year, by an act of the state government, Wyandotte (as it came to be spelled after the war) and adjacent towns Kansas City, Kansas, and Armourdale were incorporated into a single city. The governor chose the name of Kansas City, Kansas, despite the fact that the older Wyandotte was three times larger than the other two towns combined.

Directly south, through Johnson County, town centers developed in primarily agricultural communities as farmers' market areas. Farmers and other settlers were drawn to Kansas by the Homestead Act and its promise of cheap land.

In the early days, enterprise in the region was less a description of business than of a businesslike habit of mind. No one settled in early Kansas City who wasn't ready to try to build something better than what was there.

The fervent determination of early business leaders is the stuff of legend. None doubted that the fortunate site at the rivers' confluence was the mark of greatness.

One early local booster was William Gilpin, a man with the kind of colorful mix of occupations the frontier encouraged — soldier, explorer, editor and real estate developer. He predicted that by 1955 Kansas City would be a "Centropolis" with a population of 50 million people. It was inflated rhetoric, but hard work and dedicated leadership put the Kansas City region on the nation's expanding map.

When a core group of entrepreneurs set about resurrecting what was left of Kansas City, Missouri, after the Civil War, they knew they faced a formidable task. The situation didn't look promising for Kansas City. The railroad had reached St. Joseph, Missouri, before the war started and had strengthened that river town's commercial connections with the East. Business in Kansas City was almost at a standstill.

The infamous Order No. 11, issued in 1863 after Quantrill's bloody raid on nearby Lawrence, Kansas, gave citizens living outside the Union-occupied towns in Jackson, Bates and Cass counties 15 days to prove allegiance to the Union or leave the district. Families abandoned their homes and fled, terrorized by rumors and by real instances of looting and murder.

The Coates House Hotel became an emblem for what followed. Kersey Coates had gotten his hotel project built to the first floor when the war came. Union troops took it over for a stable. After the war, Coates had the debris cleaned out and began to build. When the establishment was finished, it set the tone for the era to come: spacious and ornate with all the modern conveniences, including a marble swimming pool in the basement. It had a ballroom for public functions and backrooms for private ones.

In one of those backrooms, the city's renaissance was planned over brandy and cigars by men like Coates, Robert T. Van Horn, Johnston Lykins, William Gillis, Bernard Corrigan, Thomas Swope, Kirkland Armour and others.

Three dramatic events coincided within a decade to make it happen. First, Kansas City secured a railroad bridge across the Missouri. Within the decade, 39 rail lines used Kansas City as a hub. However, the railroads' impact was greatly increased by two other forces for change: a northern shift in the cattle market and the successful introduction to Kansas of Turkey Red wheat by German Mennonites and Catholics from the Russian Volga.

During the 1870s, the market for livestock driven from Texas ranges for slaughter and shipment from Kansas City created the city's first million-dollar industry. The hardy wheat that could withstand the prairie's hot summers became another great industry. Together, beef and bread spun off many complementary businesses and built Kansas City's reputation as a commercial center of agriculture, manufacturing and distribution.

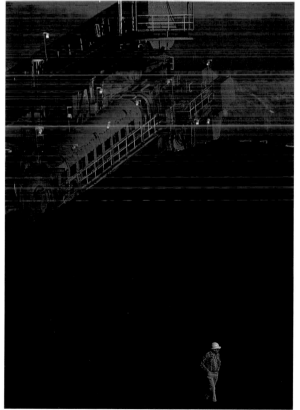

Business depends on ready energy. Traditional energy sources, such as coal (left, at Kansas City Power & Light's Iatan power plant), oil and nuclear energy generated at the Wolf Creek facility in Kansas (above), provide the region with plentiful energy at a cost below that of many other regions of the country.

In 1921 Kansas City was entering a decade of dramatic growth in many areas, especially manufacturing. Seen to the north up Broadway from Penn Valley Park were downtown's smokestacks and light haze — signs of a new economic era.

The rivers were the main highways west for travelers in the first 60 years of the nineteenth century and they made the region a center for commerce. Today the Missouri provides most of the area's drinking water, carries tons of commercial shipments each year and attracts boaters, fishermen and sightseers.

The thousands of jobs and millions of dollars generated in these sectors helped support other enterprises as well. A great entrepreneurial spirit continued, fueling new kinds of businesses. Banking and professional services, retail and construction industries grew apace. Almost overnight, the region had a richly diversified economic base and a population to match.

In the century since, this diversification has helped the area withstand larger economic forces. Inflation, recessions, even depression have dug less deeply into this region's resources than into many others because variety of enterprise sustains the economy.

Growth and government have been linked from the early days. The successful connections have often been public and private partnerships that turned the best ideas of the area's civic leadership into governmentally sanctioned, sometimes government-supported, programs. From the leadership of Robert T. Van Horn (who served as Kansas City's mayor immediately after the Civil War) to the work of elected officials representing the eight counties that make up the Mid-America Regional Council today, cooperation has been a watchword for economic progress.

Civic leaders — government officials or others — articulated community policy. The resonance of individual voices in government issues and community progress was so strong that a cursory look at Kansas City history always gives the impression of a handful of businessmen rebuilding the city during Reconstruction and guiding it thereafter. In fact, the responsibility for achievement was far more widely shared, but it is true that a single man could have enormous influence — especially if he owned a newspaper.

In the time before radio and television, newspapers were a muscular force in business, politics, indeed every aspect of community life. Editorials from the pens of newspapermen Robert Van Horn and his *Kansas City Enterprise*, Louis Hammerslough and his *Kansas City Globe*, and William

Rockhill Nelson and his *Kansas City Star* not only described, but often shaped, the region's affairs.

During the Gay Nineties, for example, when Kansas City had become the 25th-largest city in the United States, Nelson's paper, along with civic and elected officials, tried to keep the region looking ahead through the depression that followed the Wall Street panic of 1893. Farmers nationwide were outraged by falling commodity prices and rising costs; a Populist national party appealed to many of them and, on one occasion, gun-carrying farmers marched on the Kansas state capital. Then the election of Republican president William McKinley in 1896 brought a pro-business, pro-city point of view to the national scene, and the economy, including farm prices, stabilized. Kansas City began to grow again.

But the slowdown had contributed to unemployment in Kansas City; social needs were even greater than before, and no significant impact on them could be made by private relief agencies. There was fertile ground for a different kind of leadership than businessmen and civic counselors had provided. A new Democratic political organization gained strength from these circumstances and flourished among the packing houses and livestock pens of the West Bottoms where unemployment and poverty were greatest.

In a city already predisposed to listen to individuals with appealing ideas, a man with a plan was welcome. Democratic alderman James Pendergast built a strong ward loyalty based on his own informal welfare organization. Ultimately, this became the foundation of the Pendergast political machine.

Early in the twentieth century, Jim Pendergast's "Goats" and a competing faction, called "Rabbits," led the area Democratic party and thereby Kansas City politics. Jim's younger brother Tom assumed leadership in 1910 and soon consolidated the factions. For nearly 30 years, business interests had to contend with the political realities of the

The nation's second-largest rail center, Kansas City is a hub for railroads, such as the Burlington Northern (above) and Kansas City Southern Industries (right), with trains shown here delivering to Kansas City Power & Light's Hawthorn plant.

User-friendly Kansas City International Airport, located north of downtown Kansas City, is exempt from the problems many urban airports face, especially cramped capacity and noise pollution. KCI has plenty of room for the future, even for extra long runways to accommodate supersonic craft; it already serves as a designated alternate landing site for America's space shuttle. And the roar of traffic dissipates quickly over rolling countryside that surrounds the airport, thanks to progressive zoning practices that deter high-density development under flight paths.

A multibillion-dollar building boom reshaped the central city's skyline in the 1980s. It established new business corridors and brought Kansas City national attention as a company-relocation destination.

Pendergast machine which dominated city and county politics, and exerted some national influence as well.

Pendergast politics presented business with a paradox. On the one hand, beginning with saloonkeeper Jim's influence, the Pendergast name was linked to vice and gambling interests. While the machine evidently wasn't bad for business, it permitted and encouraged activities that were illegal. On the other hand, Jim Pendergast believed in civic improvements. A building boom that lasted until World War I, then picked up again after the war and continued for 10 years more, owed some of its sweep and grandeur to Pendergast money.

The city had just a few modern skyscrapers by 1910, including two in the Chicago School style: the R.A. Long Building and the Scarritt Building and Arcade. Some new hotels, including the world-class Muehlebach, were going up, along with the first moving picture theaters, automobile showrooms and other emblems of the modern era. Even with the interruption of the war, the next 20 years marked big changes.

By 1930 the city had impressive new buildings for business, including the Federal Reserve Bank Building and the new Board of Trade Building. Pleasure wasn't ignored, either. The Kansas City Club, the Pla-Mor Ballroom, fabulous theaters such as the Empire and the $4 million Loew's Midland, and hotels, such as the Phillips and the Continental, soon dotted the local map. Within the next five years, building projects transformed the heart of the region and provided a skyline admired nationwide. Moreover, the city was punctuated with lovely parks and boulevards that preserved green space from downtown to gracious residential areas.

A $40 million public works project, initiated by a "Civic Improvement Committee of 1,000" and supported by Pendergast, passed in 1931. Among the 20 projects of the Ten Year Plan were a new city hall, a flood-protection program for the Blue River and improvements throughout the parks system. New buildings at the time included the Kansas City Power & Light building, the new Jackson County Courthouse and the new Municipal Auditorium. The last two were built with concrete from Tom Pendergast's company, Ready-Mixed, as were the Nelson-Atkins Art Gallery and the runways at the new Municipal Airport, developed just across the Missouri river from downtown Kansas City.

During the Great Depression, Pendergast's national connections reportedly attracted to Kansas City a greater amount of assistance than might otherwise have been allotted. Works Progress Administration projects also provided an important source of employment and left an enduring legacy, including much of the stonework that graces the area's parks, the exquisite mosaics and other details in the Municipal Auditorium and recreational areas such as the nearly 200-acre Lee's Summit Lake.

Some historians believe this flow of federal funds buffered the city from the Depression. Others count its management by Pendergast a tragic flaw in the region's development. In any case, the control held by the Pendergast machine is almost unmatched in the history of American cities. Its influence began to unravel as federal regulations and oversight reached deeper into local politics; as the machine's own excesses (including more than 60,000 ghost voters) increased; and as Boss Tom's personal power waned with illness and the weight of gambling debts.

A business group calling itself "Forward Kansas City" foresaw new industrial energy and worked to attract new business. Reformers filled municipal offices in 1940 and held control of city government for almost 20 years. During that time, Kansas City's bond rating showed marked improvement and ambitious plans were made for growth.

Far-reaching annexation added nearly 250 square miles to the city limits of Kansas City. The metropolitan area at large was stretching still farther as an expressway program started in the late 1940s created trafficways and

Established as the Commercial Exchange before the Civil War and refocused as a grain exchange in 1869, the Kansas City Board of Trade was located at 10th and Wyandotte in 1925. The trading floor then (above) appeared serene by comparison to today's frantic activity. Now visitors to the Board of Trade building near the Country Club Plaza can watch trading of Value Line Index Futures from a gallery over the "pit," a two-story trading floor (above right).

Unusual soil conditions in pockets of land near Weston, Missouri, create one of the few places outside the Southeastern states where tobacco is grown.

Agribusiness is more than the beef and bread for which the region is famed. A local poinsettia "farm" is ready for the holiday rush. Lawn and garden companies and nurseries are some of the area's fastest-growing industries.

More than 20 important parks and municipal building projects — financed by a $40 million public works program along with federal assistance — made the 1930s a period of unexpected growth. Finished in the depths of the Depression, the stunning Art Deco Kansas City Power & Light Building at 1330 Baltimore, with its prismatic glass and automated lighting system that changes the tower's colors at night, is one of the visual reminders that Kansas City has persevered and even prospered during tough times.

thoroughfares that put suburban living within easier driving distance.

World War II stimulated the local economy almost beyond imagination, lifting it out of the Depression and carrying enterprise to new highs. Business leaders aggressively sought industrial contracts. Area manufacturing interests retooled for war, and huge new concerns located here, resulting in an explosive expansion of the work force and growth of the transportation network. For example, the Lake City Ordnance Plant spread over 3,200 acres in Jackson County and required 6,000 workers just to build. Operated as the Remington Arms Co., it served as a model for all the nation's new munitions factories and ultimately employed nearly 22,000 workers.

When Pratt and Whitney located its Engine Plant at Bannister Road and Troost Avenue, Kansas City attracted the nation's notice. People who had thought of Midwesterners as farm folk began to see that local workers could achieve outstanding results on a factory line as one Kansas City area company after another won prestigious "Army-Navy E" awards for production performance.

Attracted by all this activity, the superior labor force and ready transportation, Aluminum Co. of America put a foundry in Kansas City. The largest area defense industry, the Sunflower Ordnance Plant, occupied 10,000 acres in the Johnson County community of DeSoto, Kansas. The garment industry, already well-established, was a primary source of uniforms and other textile products during the war. New factories and changed-use spaces as well as hundreds more workers were needed to clothe and shelter America's fighting forces. For example, the Kansas City Athletic Club's dance floor became a production area for the American Fabrics Co., which produced millions of quartermaster items such as tents and ammunition cases.

As manufacturing increased, so did transportation and food processing and distribution, traditionally Kansas City's core industries. During the war, more livestock

passed through Kansas City than any other market in America, and grain dealers handled a staggering volume, close to 200 million bushels of grain annually in some years.

New industry was not the only boost to the economy; many existing companies saw their sales go up by several hundred percent. For many, the growth continued as they successfully turned their wartime production capabilities and the skills learned by workers toward peaceful pursuits and postwar profits.

It was a new era for Kansas City, but while the manufacturing plants and industrial companies had a new lease on life, by mid-century the core business areas were showing the effects of a hundred years of wear. In the 1950s suburban building accelerated in a housing boom created by the area's increased prosperity. The effects were devastating when suburbs developed farther and farther away from the traditional downtown heart of the area. Other, smaller cities also suffered as their central business districts were virtually abandoned.

In the early 1960s, under the leadership of Mayor Ilus Davis and a cadre of determined corporate leaders, Kansas City began to look toward revitalizing its downtown. Independence and Kansas City, Kansas, also tackled urban renewal projects that led to housing rehabilitation and industrial development. Smaller cities in the area began to compete aggressively for industrial and corporate enterprise.

To be successful, all these complex projects required cooperation between the public and private sectors and among governments at every level. Metropolitan-wide approaches to problem-solving began to emerge. Federal, state, county and municipal government interaction became more important than ever to maintaining an environment where business could thrive.

Today, enterprise in the region is a complex blend of individual initiative, corporate savvy, civic interaction and public and private partnerships for progress. Such

Since 1912 when the Ford Motor Company opened the auto industry's first branch plant in the Sheffield industrial district, the regional economy has benefitted from automaking. Equipment at the modern General Motors Fairfax plant in Kansas City, Kansas, (above) seems a world away from carmaking at the same plant in 1951 (right), but the dedication of area auto workers' to quality remains unchanged.

Manufacturing in the region ranges from steel at such plants as Armco Steel Corporation (above) to peanut brittle, made by hand along with other confections at the Green Mill Candy Factory, 2020 Washington, where tours take visitors through the candy-making process (right).

Built in 1966, the Federal Building is a familiar part of the downtown skyline. The federal government is the area's largest employer, pumping nearly $6 billion a year into the regional economy.

Designated as a Federal Reserve District in 1914, Kansas City has been a banking center since. The Federal Reserve Building at 925 Grand was built in 1921, and a 1985 restoration reclaimed the beautiful architectural detail of the public lobby.

partnerships have helped the metropolitan area gain recognition as one of the top ten metropolitan areas in the country in which to locate new businesses or relocate existing companies.

Federal and local partnerships are important. The federal government is the area's largest single employer and pumps nearly $6 billion annually into the local economy. Moreover, the metro area's bi-state configuration puts eight delegates from Kansas and Missouri in the U.S. House and Senate in Washington who are attentive to the needs of the greater Kansas City area.

State and local partnerships also play a key role in spurring economic development and employment opportunities throughout the metropolitan area. Helping seek and coordinate intergovernmental alliances is the Area Relations Committee, made up of representatives of each community in the metropolitan area. It operates under the aegis of the public and private leadership group known as the Kansas City Area Development Council. The council was formed in 1976 with a membership of more than 80 area businesses and 20 metropolitan cities, counties, development groups and Chambers of Commerce. It provides information and assistance to businesses and industrial concerns that are considering locating in the Kansas City area.

The Mid-America Regional Council was formed to create a forum for communication. This unusual organization represents eight counties and is led by a board of directors made up of elected officials from various government entities within the counties. A professional staff provides research to help the board address area-wide issues of enormous variety, from air quality to services for the aged, from handling hazardous materials to child care. In addition, MARC's Research Data Center makes customized economic and demographic information available to organizations in the public and private sectors.

Cities face continually changing problems; neither business nor government can meet

these challenges alone. Linking capabilities is the key to a successful future, and this region has always excelled at teamwork.

If challenges are increasing, however, so are opportunities. Only a few years ago, most metro area companies fit into a few categories: agribusiness, manufacturing, printing, assembly, distribution and service. Now biomedical research and testing, financial services and software and hardware companies are among the enterprises that look to Kansas City to be a "best for business" location.

The area's natural and man-made advantages include:

- · proximity to the nation's geographic and demographic center
- · a communications advantage in the Central Time Zone
- · the country's premier fiber optic communication system
- · major interstate highways
- · the second-busiest rail hub in the nation;
- · the nation's largest area of developed underground storage space
- · high quality real estate at relatively low lease and purchase prices
- · a large pool of educated, easily trained workers with a strong work ethic and dedication to quality.

As a result of those attributes, businesses of many kinds make up the metropolitan area's economy today. Major companies headquartered in Kansas City include Hallmark Cards, H&R Block, Butler Manufacturing, Farmland Industries, Marion Merrell Dow, Yellow Freight, Interstate Bakeries, United Telecommunications, US Sprint, Kansas City Southern Industries, DST Systems, Western Auto, Burns & McDonnell Engineering and Payless Cashways.

Other major employers include Allied Signal Aerospace Company, AT&T, Southwestern Bell, Ford Motor Co., General Motors and the University of Kansas Medical Center. More than 100 national and international associations have their headquarters in Kansas City. Employers are attracted to this area for a

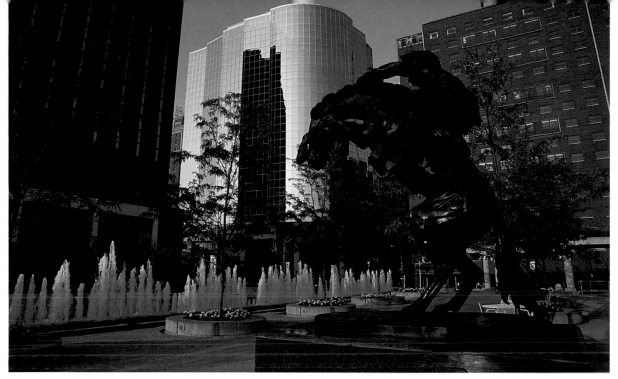

Every regional city needs a strong heart — a central place where the historical, financial, mercantile and industrial interests of surrounding communities converge. An urban renaissance is progressively restoring vitality to Kansas City's core. Ringing the Barney Allis Plaza (above), are the venerable Muehlebach Hotel (where Harry Truman woke up to find he had defeated Thomas Dewey); Twelve Wyandotte Plaza, representative of modern office buildings being constructed throughout the area; and the Allis Plaza Hotel (left), the luxury hotel whose opening in 1983 helped kick off a downtown renewal. In the foreground is the Bronco Buster by Ed Dwight.

In the mid-1840s the Wyandot tribe owned and operated a ferry across the Kansas (Kaw) River where the Lewis and Clark viaduct is today (left center in photograph). The Town of Wyandot grew up there and was renamed Kansas City, Kansas, when it merged with two smaller communities in the 1880s. Now it is a progressive community with a rich heritage, quality housing and an increasingly diverse economic base, including a brisk tourist trade. Conventions, trade shows and public events in Kansas City, Kansas, use the Reardon Civic Center (below).

Visitors are welcome guests and are an important industry in Kansas City. The Convention and Visitors Bureau of Greater Kansas City is one of the oldest in the country and there are similar bureaus in such cities as Overland Park and Kansas City, Kansas, to help meeting planners and visitors. H. Roe Bartle Hall (left), shown with a convention in progress, is part of the Kansas City Convention Center Complex, covering four blocks in the heart of downtown and in the process of major expansion. Both Democrats and Republicans have held national conventions in Kansas City, and the Future Farmers of America have met here every fall since 1928. Today more than 23,000 young delegates attend the FFA's annual meeting.

The City Market (top) at 20 East 5th has been a regional farmers' market since the 1850s. Today vendors from as far away as Texas join local sellers at more than 170 open-air stalls. On Saturdays especially, fruits, vegetables, flowers and discounted merchandise draw crowds. A multimillion-dollar River Market project now under way will create a mixed-use area along the riverfront in the historic area (above).

variety of reasons, including the competent and productive work force. One of the most popular incentives to locate here is the fact that annual office operating costs in the Kansas City area are some of the lowest in the nation.

Kansas City's oldest business sector is merchandising, and today it represents one of the fastest-growing segments of the area's economy. The third-largest industry in the area, retailing is the energy behind much of the more than $5 billion building boom that has occurred in the area since the national economic recovery began in the early 1980s. Millions of square feet of retail space have been built in the last few years, much of it in mixed-use developments linking offices and shopping.

Kansas City's per capita retail sales are among the top ten in the nation. With the population of the metropolitan area expected to grow by 22 percent, employment predicted to increase by 35 percent and the number of high-income households forecast to double by the year 2010, the outlook for retail is excellent.

Agribusiness remains a vital part of the area economy, although it bears little resemblance to the cowtown that made Kansas City virtually synonymous with "steak." Today Kansas City is at the heart of a 10-state marketing region that includes more than a third of the nation's farms and more than 40 percent of its agricultural acreage. Modern area agribusiness comprises a complex of suppliers from research scientists to hands-on feedlot operators. It includes pharmaceuticals, feeds, fertilizers, farm equipment and buildings, containers and other food production-related products, as well as all the services the industries require. The National Agri-Marketing Association and the Livestock Marketing Association are based in Kansas City, along with many livestock associations representing cattle breeders and other agriculture-related organizations, including the nation's largest agricultural fraternity.

Manufacturing continues to be important to the region, despite the national shift to a service economy. Heavy industry dominated the area's manufacturing from the development of the first smelting plants in the 1880s until the 1970s when the manufacturing sector diversified considerably. Today the top manufactured items are electrical and electronic components, plastics, greeting cards, ammunition, chemicals, prefabricated buildings, containers, pharmaceuticals and enough automobiles to keep Kansas City near the top of the nation's auto producers.

Related to manufacturing is distribution, a part of the area's business activity since the first wagon train to Santa Fe in 1825. Because it is the most centrally located of all major American cities, Kansas City offers clear advantages for distributors and ranks ninth in the nation in distribution-related businesses. It is the nation's second largest rail center and a key terminal for the trucking industry.

One of the largest foreign trade zone sites in the country is located here. The greater Kansas City Foreign Trade Zone and its three sub-zones permit goods to be brought in without clearing U.S. Customs and to be stored duty-free.

The Foreign Trade Zone means growth for Kansas City's international trade opportunities. Foreign consulates located here, as well as the international departments of several area banks, help make it possible to carry out foreign commerce directly with countries around the world. A new World Trade Center promotes trade with other countries by assisting organizations hosting foreign business and cultural delegations. Exporters and importers find warehousing for the Foreign Trade Zone and other commercial activities easy in Kansas City because of the enormous underground storage areas created by limestone mining.

Transportation is crucial to manufacturing and distribution, and Kansas City remains a major transportation center. Five interstate and eight federal highways meet here. The Missouri River's nine-foot channel provides water routes to the Gulf of Mexico and other

Business centers have risen throughout the metro area, encircling the central business district and offering attractive commercial locations ranging from densely urban to rolling rural sites. Their names are like addresses to Kansas Citians: Commerce Complex, Crown Center, Penn Valley, the Plaza, Corporate Woods, Blue Ridge and Rock Creek. A major commercial center in southern Overland Park, Kansas, Corporate Woods (above left) and the Renaissance buildings (above right) are part of the rapidly growing College Boulevard corridor. Northland-based businesses find modern homes near the airport (right). New companies are locating in the eastern areas, joining established ones such as Missouri Public Service Company (below), headquartered in Raytown, Missouri.

Government and business partnerships are important to regional development. A good example is the Linwood Shopping Center, developed with federal grants and private investments on the site of an empty hospital, to reclaim a broad section of the central city for productive commerce. The Linwood Center is one of the chief reasons Kansas City was named an All-America City by the National Municipal League and USA Today.

world ports. Kansas City International Airport has direct flights to European capitals and provides direct and connecting service to locations throughout the world.

Railroading continues to be important. Kansas City Southern Industries is headquartered here. The legendary Atchison, Topeka & Santa Fe Railroad, immortalized in song, is today a "steel freeway" connecting the nation's two busiest rail centers, Chicago and Kansas City. Thanks to the vision of William Barstow Strong in the 1880s, the Santa Fe put down a straight line from Kansas City to Chicago, ignoring the wisdom of the day, which was to weave track through the countryside to traffic-rich smaller communities. The resulting ability to move through-traffic fast helped build Kansas City as a distribution center. Today railroading is a complex blend of services, including trailer/container "intermodal" units designed to compete with the trucking industry.

Transmitting information — another kind of distribution — benefits from Kansas City's central location. A well-educated work force and the presence of colleges and universities with research capabilities also have boosted the communications industry and made Kansas City a communications hub.

In 1943 Midwest Research Institute established a regional science base that would allow industry to convert war contracts into lasting economic growth. Since then Kansas City has steadily advanced its potential and built its reputation as a sophisticated technology center, with more than 1,000 area companies involved in high technology and research.

Various organizations support fledgling companies in this relatively new industry. Situated on the campus of the University of Missouri-Kansas City is the Center for Business Innovation, a small business incubator assisting high-tech start-ups. The Silicon Prairie Technology Association represents companies and universities involved with the advanced technology industry. One of only three trade associations in the United States

that represent high-tech members, Silicon Prairie has grown from six founders in 1986 to hundreds of member companies today. Cooperation is important to the growth of a cutting-edge industry, and Kansas City has become a high-tech center in large part because of programs and ideas that connect participants across institutional boundaries and even state lines.

Already the area has become a telecommunications industry center, with nearly 150 companies employing nearly three percent of the area's work force. Because Kansas City is the hub for fiber optic networks around the region and to both coasts, the most advanced technology for communications systems is available here. Manufacturers produce components for electronic equipment of all kinds, including computers assembled in plants all over the world.

Telecommunications giant US Sprint is headquartered here, and the metropolitan area is an important link in AT&T's nationwide network. In addition to lightwave routes, many of AT&T's telemarketing, manufacturing and distribution functions are located here, making the company a major area employer. Other major corporations such as Montgomery Ward & Co., Federal Express Corporation and USA 800 have located telemarketing and telephone customer service operations in the area; DST, a subsidiary of homegrown Kansas City Southern Industries, has its primary information processing center in Kansas City, serving the financial industry with record-keeping and data processing functions.

Although agriculture and manufacturing were dominant industries in the region's early years, after World War II, the service sector became increasingly important and accounting, law and brokerage firms prospered. These services now represent the largest and fastest-growing element of the region's economic mix.

Financial institutions exemplified the growth of the service sector as they continued

Merchants were some of the area's first settlers and retailing is still a major economic force in the region where per-capita retail sales rank in the nation's top ten. From regional malls such as Independence Center on I-70 (above) to craft boutiques and fairs, shopping is crucial to Kansas City's bottom line.

Revitalization in urban centers depends on a good mix of retail opportunities and offices. The Town Pavilion provides three levels of downtown shopping at the 38-story AT&T Town Pavilion building at 11th and Main.

Shoppers who attend auctions likely will be listening to a graduate of the Missouri Auction School, the largest and oldest institution of its kind in the nation. Founded in 1905, the school is located in the Livestock Exchange building (1600 Genessee) and is staffed by professional auctioneers from all over the nation who come to Kansas City to teach their specialties from thoroughbreds to estate jewelry to business liquidations.

Shopping districts such as the Brookside Shops (established in 1919) combine the feel of a quaint village with contemporary merchandise and services. Brookside's gaslights are the only functioning commercial ones left in the city and make the area (63rd and Wornall) one of a handful of gaslight districts in the country.

to expand; by 1921 Kansas City ranked fifth in volume of bank clearings. Several Insurance companies were formed and grew into national and international organizations. Among these were Kansas City Life and Business Men's Assurance, both local companies that grew through offering a range of financial services.

Once Kansas City had secured a Federal Reserve bank in 1914, the number of federal agencies in the city skyrocketed. During the Depression, an enormous number of agencies were created as part of President Franklin D. Roosevelt's New Deal, meant to address everything from employment issues to beautification. By 1939, more than 100 federal offices were located in the metropolitan area. This buildup and the attendant volume of employees and work required a new post office in 1932, across from Union Station, and a new

federal building in 1938. In the 1960s federal social programs encouraged another expansion of the local federal work force and a move to another building. In the early 1970s Kansas City became one of ten federal regional centers, an intermediate headquarters for most federal agencies functioning in Missouri, Kansas, Iowa and Nebraska.

Whether or not the region is located on a mythical "Axis of Intensity," as William Gilpin once said, it's certain that hard work and determination have paid off in the city's economic life. Kansas City is again being hailed as a "city of the future." In recent years, the region has regularly been featured in the national business press as a "boom city" and as a desirable site for locations and relocations of national or regional operations. This growing prominence is testament to the value of life not on the edge, but in the middle.

Sports is a multimillion-dollar industry here with professional or college teams in football, baseball, basketball, hockey and soccer drawing spectators from several states. The region is also hometown headquarters for Big Eight Basketball, the National Association of Intercollegiate Athletics, the Fellowship of Christian Athletes and the National Collegiate Athletic Association. The NCAA's new visitors' center (above) is an important stop for fans of collegiate sports.

Sports facilities include the $71 million Harry S Truman Sports Complex, the world's only side-by-side baseball and football stadium, and the $12 million Kemper Arena (right). An award-winning structure in the historic West Bottoms, Kemper has been the site of such special events as National Figure Skating Championships and the NCAA Final Four basketball tournament.

When famed explorer Sir Henry M. Stanley was a writer for the St. Louis Democrat, he visited Kansas City and called it the "most religious city in the world." Today religion is important spiritually and economically. Three faiths have world headquarters here: the Reorganized Church of the Latter Day Saints, the Nazarene Church and Unity School of Christianity (above). All three have large international publishing concerns which produce millions of pieces of printed materials annually.

First in the nation in underground storage space, Kansas City has miles of naturally climate-controlled storage in the planned caves left from limestone mining. These facilities contribute to a highly successful Foreign Trade Zone where duty-free storage encourages development of foreign markets. Increasingly, Kansas City is a center for international business with operations of more than 40 foreign concerns located in the metro area.

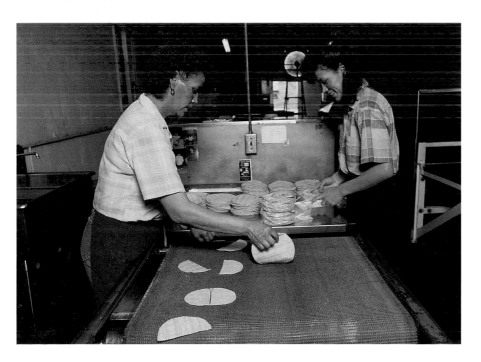

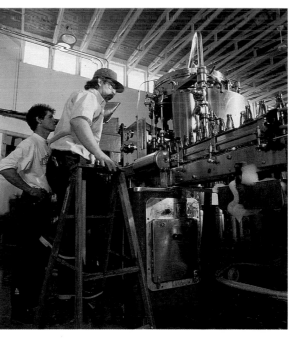

More than 90 percent of the region's enterprise can be classified as small businesses, and a high percetage of these are family-owned, such as El Tacquito Manufacturing (far left), which produces tortillas for restaurants. Boulevard Beer (left), established in 1988, was the first new brewery to open in the Kansas City area since Prohibition.

Kansas City area public companies, such as Sealright, a 150-year-old container manufacturer, have strong records on the nation's stock exchanges. Investors worldwide are familiar with the names of such Kansas City-based companies as United Telecommunications, Yellow Freight System, H &R Block and Marion Merrell Dow.

The region capitalized on its central location when business depended on transportation. Now that communication is a key to progress, location in a central time zone is a wonderful asset and telecommunications has become a major area industry. US Sprint's national operations control center (above) is the "master control" of the only nationwide, all-digital, fiber optic telecommunications network. This new hub has a legacy from Kansas City's earlier status as a rail hub: fiber optic cables are buried along the region's myriad railroad rights-of-way.

The metro area is a research and manufacturing center for the most advanced communications technology, including fiber optics. To maintain a competitive edge, research and development are critical. The area boasts Midwest Research Institute, one of the nation's top private scientific institutions; 13 colleges and universities; and more than 1,000 companies involved in advanced technology and research.

(far right) Evening light touches downtown buildings (seen from the southwest) with gold and jewel-like tones. The twinkle of Kansas City on the bluffs is said to have been the inspiration for Oz in Frank Baum's famous tale.

Creativity

Kansas City is home to us.
Our presence here is not extracurricular —
it's an equal exchange.
Kansas City embraces the arts
with open arms.

Judith Jamison
Artistic Director
Alvin Ailey American Dance Theater

Art Meets Life

Celebrations of Kansas City's best-known contribution to music abound. Events such as the Kansas City Jazz Festival and the 18th and Vine Heritage Jazz Festival draw local and national musicians and fans.

(opening) The Nelson-Atkins Museum of Art holds one of the finest collections of Oriental art in the western world, memorable European and American collections, and is committed to building a notable collection of contemporary sculpture.

(right) The Nelson Museum's Creative Art Center provides educational programming for all ages from tots to adults. A children's sidewalk art project created this alfresco affirmation.

"D azzling records are set in sales rooms, but the real life of art goes on quietly elsewhere," *New York Times* art editor John Russell once observed. He could have been describing Kansas City, where art is part of real life, every day.

Kansas City's creative life is exuberant and unpretentious. It crosses many lines — ethnicity, age, education, talent — and draws people together. Even the forms of expression mingle. Sometimes crossing artistic forms has created amazing hybrids. Two that have been a lasting gift of joy from Kansas City to the world are Kansas City jazz and Mickey Mouse.

Jazz mixed several musical styles with hot times and got a cool sound. Local artist Walt Disney mixed line drawings, theater, music and magic and got Mickey Mouse, the world's foremost cartoon personality. Together they symbolize the forms that creativity in Kansas City seems to take: upbeat, easy to like, open to all.

The humanizing, glorifying spirit that erupts when art meets life is everywhere in this city. Free concerts in parks and parking lots, in shopping centers and on the steps of public buildings; sculpture in the parks, in malls, downtown, in residential neighborhoods, in commercial office developments; fountains everywhere — more than in any other city in the world. There's no way to move through the city, even on a rush-to-work day, and not be exposed to artistic achievements.

Those who want to go the step further to seek out culture more formally find it abundant. Kansas City is home to one of the country's top eight general art museums, one

of the nation's finest regional symphonies and more professional theaters than any city of comparable size in the United States. It boasts one of the few opera companies in the world singing in English; a splendid ballet company; a busy gallery scene; and world-class performing arts facilities.

Warmly supported by the community, arts organizations and cultural activities can count on enthusiastic audiences, volunteers and patrons. Thousands of volunteers contribute nearly a quarter of a million hours annually to support cultural activities, and area businesses contribute millions of dollars in goods and services to help the arts succeed.

Recognizing that creative endeavor knows few boundaries, the states of Missouri and Kansas are looking at ways they can mutually devote more resources to the arts throughout the region. And the Kansas City Stabilization Program, a collaborative effort between local business and community leaders and the National Arts Stabilization Fund, is a $4.4 million program to strengthen the financial position and managerial skills of local arts institutions.

Culture is good business in Kansas City. About a million out-of-town visitors visit museums, historic sites and attend performing arts events each year. The economic impact is enormous — more than $85 million annually — but at least as important is the value of cultural attractions and artistic endeavor to the area's quality of life for residents and visitors both.

Business blends with creative endeavor in countless ways as companies sponsor programs in both the performing and visual arts, commission original pieces and underwrite performances.

Considered one of the eight best art museums in America, the Nelson Museum continues to develop its fine collections and innovative programming through a world-class curatorial staff and generous local patrons. The Nelson also welcomes many major traveling exhibits and has mounted its own acclaimed touring shows.

Innovative efforts to bring arts to children include the Kansas City chapter of Young Audiences, which gives children and families reduced ticket prices for performances ranging from children's theater to the Lyric Opera. Then there's Kaleidoscope, an innovative art and creativity experience for school-age children sponsored by Hallmark Cards. If these programs and the many others that exist are any indication, the future of the arts is safe in Kansas City.

Arts education is important throughout the region. Every public school district and each independent school boasts a thriving arts program; in addition, students in the Kansas City, Missouri, schools can choose to attend a Performing Arts magnet school. Area colleges and universities offer majors in the arts, and Kansas City is home to the renowned Kansas City Art Institute.

No one needs to be a student of the arts to appreciate cultural life here. People of all ages and interests find plenty to enjoy.

The Nelson-Atkins Museum of Art is the most distinguished art museum between the Great Lakes and the Pacific Ocean and is usually ranked in the top eight museums in the country. Among its holdings are one of the most treasured Oriental art collections in the western world and a major collection of more than 50 works by Henry Moore on permanent loan from the Hall Family Foundations. The institution's original collection was endowed by a bequest from William Rockhill Nelson, and the magnificent structure to house it was built with Nelson's bequest and contributions from the estate of Mary Atkins on the site of Nelson's home, Oak Hall.

The Kansas City Art Institute, founded in 1885, is the oldest arts institution in Kansas City. The private, four-year college trains artists and designers and is the only college of art and design between Chicago and the West Coast. Alumni such as Walt Disney and Robert Rauschenberg have made lasting impressions on American life. The Institute offers regularly changing exhibits. In the

planning stage is the Kemper Museum of Contemporary Art and Design, a gift to the Institute to be built on the former site of the Conservatory of Music across the street from the current campus.

The Kansas City Artists Coalition, formed in 1973 as a contemporary center for the arts, presents exhibitions, performances, lectures and readings. More than 40 area galleries display the work of regional artists, as well as national and international talents. Galleries and antique shops are clustered in some of the city's restored areas, such as Westport, where a number of Kansas City's oldest buildings house restaurants and shops; the River Market area; and midtown along State Line Road.

While the visual arts can bring out people — sometimes thousands a day for an exhibit at the Nelson — the way to put a really big crowd together in Kansas City is to strike up a tune. From dignified string quartets to down-home, foot-stomping country fiddle, music is in the air year round.

The Kansas City Symphony, considered one of the finest regional symphonies in the nation, has built a sold-out following by taking classical music to the people. The Symphony plays in parks and hotel lobbies and on museum lawns. Under the baton of music director and conductor William McGlaughlin, the Symphony has taken an upbeat approach to "good music," bringing in pop stars and poets as guest artists, along with some of the finest classical musicians in the world.

Another classical music group, the Friends of Chamber Music, has grown in only a little more than a decade from a small group of "friends" to a powerful arts organization with a full season of world-renowned performers, ranging from quartets to large chamber orchestras. The Conservatory of Music at the University of Missouri-Kansas City originated in 1906 as a busy music school. In 1957 it merged with the University of Kansas City, now the University of Missouri-Kansas City. Today fine musicians teach and train at the

The Strawberry Hill Museum and Cultural Center (720 North 4th) in Kansas City, Kansas, occupies the 1873 home of railroad magnate James A. Cruise. Opened in 1988, the museum (above) houses Croatian artifacts and historical data and is important to maintaining ethnic traditions in one of the region's oldest neighborhoods.

(above) Small wonder that visitors from all over seek out the Toy and Miniature Museum, the only museum of its kind in the Midwest. Called by The New York Times "one of the world's 10 tiny treats," the museum offers one of the best such collections in the world. It houses miniatures, dollhouses (from 1840) and toys and also displays traveling exhibitions in a restored 1911 mansion (5235 Oak) recently expanded by a $2.3 million addition.

(above) "East Gate Piece" by Dale Eldridge, well-known artist and Kansas City Art Institute graduate, welcomes visitors to the school which also counts among its illustrious graduates Walt Disney and Robert Rauschenberg.

(left) The main facility of the Kansas City Museum is the 1910 mansion called Corinthian Hall, 3218 Gladstone, built by lumberman Robert A. Long. Today the museum of science and regional history includes a planetarium and a 1910 drugstore interior with an operating soda fountain. Temporary exhibits are featured in the museum's satellite facility in the Town Pavilion (1111 Main).

97

Count Basie on Vine Street recalls the genius of Kansas City jazz. The Kansas City jazz style, developed in jam sessions in nearly a hundred Kansas City clubs from the 1920s through the late 1930s, was a combination of swinging dance beats and the urge musicians felt to improvise. Today jam sessions and jazz festivals attract outstanding musicians. Several organizations, including the Kansas City Jazz Ambassadors and the Kansas City Jazz Commission, work to promote jazz and organize events, particularly during Kansas City Jazz and Heritage Month in August.

Conservatory, which offers more than 350 concerts and recitals by students and professionals each year.

Despite the prominence of Kansas City's classical music scene, the city is without a doubt best known for another musical form: jazz. In the 1920s, '30s and '40s jazz greats such as Bennie Moten, Jay McShann, Lester Young, Charlie "Bird" Parker, Joe Turner, Count Basie and Mary Lou Williams made Kansas City a special place on music's map.

For a red-hot decade during the 1930s, the area immortalized by Count Basie as "Twelfth Street and Vine" was a 'round-the-clock carnival.

The Mutual Musicians Foundation, today a national historic landmark at 1823 Highland, has been a jazz mecca for more than 50 years. On weekends, musicians old and young still get together for late-night jam sessions. Today the Charlie Parker Memorial Foundation promotes the study of music and dance by young black students, offering lessons on a sliding fee basis or by scholarship so that no aspiring youngster is turned away.

Kansas City is rediscovering its jazz heritage. Clubs and festivals create opportunities for the public to hear jazz live and for musicians from all over the country to meet and jam. The Kansas City Jazz Commission maintains a Jazz Hot Line, hosts the annual Kansas City Jazz Festival and organizes Jazz Lovers' Pub Crawls.

Kansas City's music lovers are a broad-based bunch. They pack the city's classical, jazz, pop, rock and country venues year-round. The summer's outdoor concert season — from the Brown Bag lunchtime concerts on downtown's Barney Allis Plaza to Crown Center's Summer on the Square free concerts every Friday night —may be the region's biggest melting pot, attracting more diverse crowds than even sporting events. Big outdoor concerts are a tradition in Kansas City. In 1951 the city committed itself to a large, permanent, open-air facility called Starlight Theater. Not only is it a venue for major musical

events, but it also is one of the best-known summer theaters in the United States today.

Indoors or out, the region values theater. With 12 professional theaters in operation, Kansas City is home to more professional theater companies than any city of comparable size in the United States and ranks third in the nation for professional theaters per capita.

Since its debut as a university summer program in 1964, the Missouri Repertory Theatre has earned a national reputation by staging classics and contemporary plays and bringing actors and directors of national and international stature to Kansas City.

The Theater League brings professional touring companies in new and restaged plays and musicals to the 2,800-seat Midland Center for the Performing Arts downtown and to Johnson County Cultural Education Center's state-of-the art theater. The not-for-profit Theater League also produces its own, more intimate, off-Broadway-style theater in the Quality Hill Playhouse.

The American Heartland Theatre emphasizes fun with comedies, musicals and murder mysteries. Located in Crown Center, the Heartland is one of only two professional theater companies located in a retail center. The second, also located in Crown Center, is The Coterie, a children's theater of regional renown.

Smaller Equity and non-Equity companies are also thriving. Waldo Astoria and Tiffany's Attic playhouses, two of America's most successful dinner theaters, feature nationally-known guest artists and have entertained four million theater-goers with substantial buffets and light comedies. In 1991 the Waldo Astoria closed to be reborn in a Johnson County shopping district as The New Theatre.

Because of high New York production costs, small, regional theaters such as Kansas City's Unicorn Theater offer excellent try-outs for adventuresome programming. Kansas City is known as a good place to test new plays. Additionally, about a dozen commu-

Under music director William McGlaughlin, the Kansas City Symphony has found new audiences for its regular series and for a wide variety of other concerts such as the NightLights pops series in community settings throughout the metroplex. The region's largest orchestra also tours within the six-state region.

Music lovers find a wide range in Kansas City, including classical and chamber music, country and rock 'n roll, blues and jazz. Clubs and concerts keep live music readily available.

The Mutual Musicians Foundation building in the historic 18th & Vine District is a gathering place for professional musicians who jam there day and night. Originally the Black Musicians Union Local 627, this organization has encouraged the careers of many jazz legends since its founding in 1904.

For more than 50 years, the Plaza Art Fair has annually transformed the Country Club Plaza into an outdoor art gallery for a weekend in late September.

nity theater groups offer the area's professional and non-professional players opportunities on stage.

Dance in Kansas City has ties to two of the century's most influential dance masters. The State Ballet of Missouri (formerly the Kansas City Ballet) has as its artistic director Todd Bolender, a protégé of the late George Balanchine. Bolender's leadership has brought the State Ballet to regional prominence and national recognition. The company maintains a repertoire of more than 40 ballets that showcase the fresh, athletic approach of the dancers. Each season the Ballet presents fall, winter and spring performances as well as a beloved version of the holiday classic *The Nutcracker Suite.*

The Ballet cultivated a lively relationship with Alvin Ailey, the late choreographer, whose company appeared in joint performances with the State Ballet. The Friends of Alvin Ailey, a not-for-profit community organization formed in 1984, provides an ongoing "second home" for the Alvin Ailey American Dance Theater in Kansas City.

The Westport Ballet Theater Company brings dance to the public through free public performances in theaters and in open-air public places. The State Ballet, Westport Ballet, City in Motion and many area dance studios and companies headed by performing and former professional dancers have teaching programs that prepare young dancers for careers as well as assure the appreciation of dance in Kansas City.

Local celebrations combine all forms of the arts as they bring to life the traditions and special talents of the many peoples who settled here. The Annual Kansas City Indian Club Pow Wow brings native Americans of many tribes together at the Wyandotte County Fairgrounds in July to compete in dance and other skills. During Hispanic Heritage Week in early September, Kansas City's Hispanic community invites everyone to share in a merry and colorful celebration of its culture with authentic music, dancing and

cuisine. In August, the Ethnic Enrichment Festival is a three-day event honoring ethnic groups throughout the region. Kansas City, Kansas, alone has more than two dozen annual celebrations, earning it the nickname of the "City of Festivals."

In addition to many other regular ethnic festivals, some local events celebrate the area's history. For example, the yearly Heritage Art Show at the Kansas City Museum depicts Kansas City history. Independence, Missouri, remembers its contributions as the starting place for the Santa Fe, California and Oregon trails with Santa-Cali-Gon Days on Independence Square each fall. August is Jazz and Heritage Month with concerts, exhibits and events such as the 18th and Vine Heritage Festival that pay tribute to Kansas City's jazz legacy.

Living history combines many forms of creative expression. Among the area's more than 25 museums and historic sites are several that offer living history programs. Over 70 percent of the visitors to the area are attracted to museums and historic sites.

The life and times of Harry S Truman are recalled in the office and courtroom in the historic Jackson County Courthouse, Independence, Missouri, where Truman served as administrative judge for the county before he went on first to the United States Senate and ultimately to the presidency. Not far away in Grandview, Missouri, is the farm home where Truman said he "spent the best years" of his life. Now a Registered National Historic Landmark, the little white frame house and its outbuildings reconstruct an important period in the life of one of America's best-loved presidents.

Old Shawnee Town is a recreation of a Kansas pioneer community with vintage and reconstructed buildings that depict life in Gum Springs — later Shawnee — in the mid-nineteenth century. Shoal Creek in Hodge Park north of the Missouri River is a reconstruction of a frontier village of the 1800s that includes log cabins and a stone grist mill.

The National 3-Dimensional Art Show in Lenexa, Kansas each May displays 350 works from artists in 50 states.

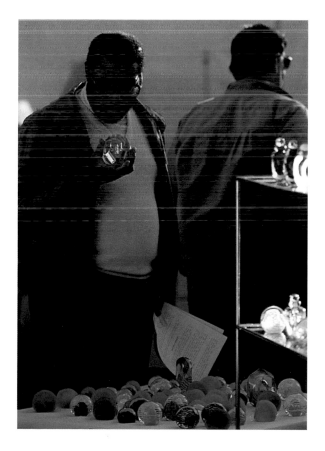

(left) Annual art shows draw exhibitors and visitors from all over the nation. So popular are these events that almost every area of the city has an annual art fair or crafts show, including Art Westport, the National Wildlife Art Show and the Heritage Art Show at the Kansas City Museum.

Artist Jack Garnier (above) works on a mural for the RLDS Temple, scheduled for completion in 1993 next to the RLDS Auditorium, the world church headquarters in Independence, Missouri.

In 1978 artist Christo covered two-and-a-half miles of paths in Loose Park with saffron-colored nylon. "Wrapped Walkways," joined his California "Running Fences" as one of the artist's most widely-known works. For several splendid days, the walks glittered under blue October skies (left) and delighted thousands of park visitors.

Harry S Truman asked Kansas City artist and longtime friend, Thomas Hart Benton (right), to paint murals for the Truman Library in Independence. Benton created "Independence and the Opening of the West," completed in 1961. The murals poignantly reflect the original American dream.

The past becomes a cultural experience in museums where the area's heritage is preserved as energetically as its present is enriched. The Kansas City Museum of History and Science in Corinthian Hall, the ornate 70-room mansion built by lumber baron Robert A. Long in 1910, houses more than 250,000 regional artifacts, an American Indian collection and a clothing and textile collection. The museum emphasizes interactive programming.

The Johnson County Historical Museum in Shawnee traces the development of the area through daily artifacts from diaries to weapons; farther south in Edgerton is the Lanesfield School Historic site, a one-room stone schoolhouse that is the only structure left of the town of Lanesfield, which served as a mail stop on the Santa Fe Trail.

The Black Archives of Mid-America, located in the historic 18th & Vine District, is a collection of documents, photographs and objects relating to the experience of black Americans in the region. A $200-million plan by the non-profit Black Economic Development Union includes expansion of the Archives, an International Jazz Hall of Fame and a museum dedicated to players from the Negro baseball leagues.

Another unusual tribute is the Liberty Memorial Museum, the only museum and archive in the country dedicated exclusively to the preservation and study of World War I. The Museum is located at the base of the 200-foot Liberty Memorial tower topped by the "Torch of Liberty"; it houses artifacts and memorabilia, including a replica of a battlefield trench. On the opposite side of the tower, Memory Hall contains paintings by various artists, a poster collection and powerful murals by local artist Daniel MacMorris.

On the other end of the scale of size from the Liberty Memorial guarded by its giant Sphinx figures are the tiny houses and tinier objects of the Toy and Miniature Museum of Kansas City, a collection of miniatures, antique dollhouses and antique toys in a restored and expanded mansion on the Univer-

The annual Renaissance Festival benefits the Kansas City Art Institute. For seven weekends in the fall, thousands of visitors flock to a sixteenth-century village recreated in leafy glades adjacent to the Agricultural Hall of Fame in Bonner Springs, Kansas, to mingle with 3,000 costumed artisans, entertainers, food sellers and jousters.

Living history depicts daily life at Missouri Town 1855 in Fleming Park at Lake Jacomo. A recreated antebellum farming community, Missouri Town is made up of original structures moved from many Missouri locations to the park in order to demonstrate life in rural Western Missouri before the Civil War.

(above) Art is everywhere in Kansas City, often providing an unexpectedly rich background to other activities. (left) A visiting mariachi band from Seville, Spain, Kansas City's sister city, entertains passersby on the Country Club Plaza beneath the Giralda Tower, a replica of the famed tower in Seville.

sity of Missouri-Kansas City campus.

The Truman Library and Museum has been called one of the most accessible of presidential libraries. It houses millions of documents, archives and memorabilia, including a presidential limousine and the table on which the United Nations Charter was signed, and has a mural by nationally known Kansas City artist Thomas Hart Benton. Harry and Bess Truman are buried in the courtyard. The Truman National Landmark District was created by the city of Independence and the Department of the Interior to preserve the neighborhood where Harry Truman lived — and where he took his nightly walks when he came home to Independence from the White House. The district includes the area on both sides of Delaware Street from the Truman home to the presidential library.

Not far away is the 1859 Jail Museum, which was used in the Civil War by both the North and South. Frank James served time there, but Frank's more-famous brother, Jesse, earned a museum all his own. The Jesse James Bank Museum, located on the Old Town Square in Liberty, Missouri is the site of the world's first daylight bank robbery, which was pulled off by the James Gang in 1866. The museum has intact all the furnishings and equipment that were there when Jesse came to make his "withdrawal."

Homes-as-museums are important to the area's sense of tradition and are treasured not only for their educational value but also as sites for public and private entertainments.

The John Wornall House is a charming restoration of the 1858 Georgian home that exemplifies the life of a well-to-do-farmer just before the Civil War.

The Bingham-Waggoner Estate in Independence is the restored 1855 estate and mansion that was once home to artist George Caleb Bingham. Also in Independence is the Vaile Mansion, a 31-room Victorian extravaganza which preserves the opulence of the Second Empire Style, interpreted for life in the Midwest. Other preserved homes include the

In the theater of the Johnson County Community College Cultural Education Center (above), the Youth Symphony plays a spring concert. This orchestra and the Junior Youth Symphony provide talented young musicians opportunities to perform symphonic literature.

(right) The Martin City Melodrama & Vaudeville Co. offers boisterous productions in a small theater (13440 Holmes) with wooden benches and a floor strewn with peanut shells dropped by the audience. The shows recall entertainments popular when Martin City was established in 1887 (as a railroad stop first called Tilden, then renamed for himself by Edward Martin, one of the town's founders).

The Missouri Repertory Theatre's professional productions of plays represent the full range of dramatic literature and are widely renowned for not only acting and direction but for outstanding staging. Since 1979, The Rep has been at home in the state-of-the-art 733-seat Helen F. Spencer Theatre on the campus of the University of Missouri Kansas City. Although The Rep is an independent corporation, it maintains a commitment to university theater training programs.

The $23-million Cultural Education Center at Johnson County Community College, opened in 1990, provides several theaters, including the 1,400-seat all-purpose Yardley Hall, art exhibition space, classrooms and offices. A series of brick sculptures adorns the lobby area.

The Lyric Opera of Kansas City, dedicated to producing opera as theater and in English, has been in the forefront of the regional opera movement since its beginning in 1958. It is considered one of the nation's major opera companies. The oldest touring opera program in the Midwest, the Lyric takes full-scale productions on the road each year.

The Intimate America Heartland Theatre, located in Crown Center, has no seat more than 12 rows from the stage. The theater offers American standards and innovative new plays.

Strawberry Hill Museum and Cultural Center, Grinter House, the Mahaffie Farmstead, the Alexander Majors House, Longview Farm and the Thomas Hart Benton Home and Studio.

These homes and museums, like other efforts made here to hold on to the best of the past, reflect a universal respect for both discipline and dreams and an unjaded appreciation of the artistic potential in any individual's best work.

Today these values persist and recur in the creative life of the region. They surface in myriad varieties of art and craft, from gala symphony performances to simple rag rugs hooked the way pioneer women did six generations ago. These values inspire artists and audiences alike and give Kansas City a cultural dimension of uncommon richness and depth.

The annual production of "The Nutcracker Suite" by the State Ballet of Missouri is one of Kansas City's beloved holiday traditions.

For nearly 20 years, Kansas City's two dinner theaters, Tiffany's Attic and the Waldo Astoria (now known as The New Theatre), have served up over 200 productions and more than 1,400 tons of beef to more than four million theater goers — making the operations two of the most successful such theaters in the nation.

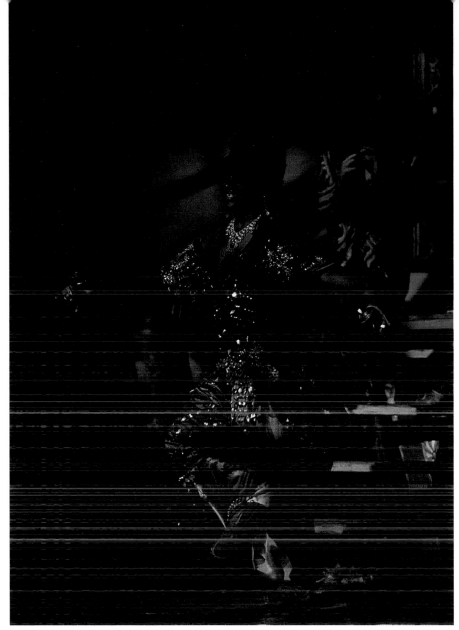

(above) Every dancer has to begin at the beginning, and the Kansas City area has dance training of many kinds for people of all ages.

(above) At the annual Ethnic Enrichment festival, the dances of India mesmerize visitors. The three-day event celebrates the colorful heritage of the region's many ethnic groups. (right) Many of the 57 American Indian tribes represented in the region meet at annual pow wows where traditional tribal dances are high points in the festivities.

(above) The State Ballet of Missouri, under the artistic direction of Todd Bolender, has achieved national recognition performing important historical and contemporary works with an ambitious home and touring season, and a second-home residency in St. Louis.

(above right) Since 1984 City in Motion Dance Theater has been a regional center for the advancement of modern dance. In addition to a professional company, City in Motion offers an educational Dance Center and a Children's Dance Theater, an outgrowth of a scholarship program for disadvantaged youths.

(right) The internationally famous, multiracial Alvin Ailey American Dance Theater has established a second home in Kansas City and has served as a catalyst for both artistic and civic support of dance in the area. In 1984 the Kansas City Friends of Alvin Ailey, Inc. was formed with funding provided by local business and private donors to secure the ongoing presence of the company here. Public performances, new works and educational outreach, including workshops and school performances, are all part of the company's residency. An innovative summer program, Aileycamp, focuses on at-risk students to develop academic and interpersonal skills.

(far right) Since 1950 summer in Kansas City has meant Starlight Theatre, one of the country's most highly regarded summer stock theaters. The 8,000-seat outdoor amphitheater in Swope Park presents Broadway musicals and contemporary concerts.

Vitality

Kansas City has always been
a great sports town.
This is outdoor country.
I like the change the seasons
bring our recreational life.
But best of all are the people.
We work together and get things done.

Tom Watson
Golf Professional

All in the Game

"Play hard!" is the matching maxim to "work hard." Kansas Citians — like this member of the local polo team — take both to heart.

(opening) Opening Day for the Kansas City Royals baseball club at Royals Stadium is an official holiday on the emotional calendar of most Kansas Citians. Even those who aren't at the game mark it as the real first day of summer.

(right) In the spirit of old-time band concerts, tens of thousands of people take picnics and blankets to free Friday night concerts in Crown Center's Summer on the Square series.

Choose a phrase that best describes most people in the Kansas City region and "good sports" likely would be it. Not that they don't compete with an in-your-face intensity. They do. Even so, people here are still good sports — partly from their simple love of a game, but mostly from the pervasive spirit of fair play found everywhere from the T-ball field to the golf course.

It's no wonder that Kansas City is called the "Sports Capital of Mid-America." Residents love games and competitions of all sorts, and put a considerable premium on fresh air and outdoor activities. Whether spectators or participants, in organized sports or simple relaxation, they like to be active.

Active lifestyles are the flip side of the business drive that built the region. Indolence wasn't part of the baggage settlers brought with them, and those who have come after have continued to keep busy.

In fact, around here the universal greeting "How are you?" is met with the reply, "Keeping busy." Sometimes, the greeting itself goes: "Keeping busy?" The possible answers are: "Real busy!" (local jargon for "Everything is just fine!") or "Too busy!" (which means "I'm really stressed!") or "Not as busy as I'd like to be!" (another way to say "Times are tough").

This doesn't mean the area is filled with workaholics. On the contrary, "keeping busy" can mean having fun. As strong as the work ethic is in this part of the country, it is balanced by the urge to play. Weather permitting, people take to the parks, the streets, the playgrounds, the athletic fields and their own backyards at every chance for virtually every

kind of recreation. If work makes the heart of America beat, play keeps its spirit light.

There's a playfulness and a fundamental love of life in evidence all over the region, every day. Small things give it away, like the way people move through the day appreciatively, as if they had time enough to enjoy the passage. It's a busy — but not frantic — city.

One 1990 study ranked Kansas City among the nation's top ten cities for *pace of life*, as measured by such standards as speedy response to questions, time taken to complete a given task and number of people wearing watches.

If they stopped to think about it Kansas, Citians could easily explain the study's findings. To local folks, those standards measure things more important than pace: *courtesy* (prompt response when addressed); *diligence* (identify what needs to be done and do it); and *responsibility* (don't be late).

Actually, the pace of life in Kansas City is a blend that could be expected, knowing that Boston emigrants and southern gentry got together to help build a town. The result is gracious ease with a heavy dash of salty determination; things get done and done well, usually in style.

Generally shared, if unspoken, are ancient priorities. A time to plant and a time to reap. A time to pull down and a time to build up. A time to scatter stones and a time to gather them. A time to work and a time to play. People here take a moment to "smell the roses." They look openly at their surroundings and each other. Even on city streets, strangers smile and speak. It's the behavior of people who have energy to share. It's a vital spirit.

The spirit is certainly easiest to see in sports, long a boon to this healthy city of hills,

Long summers mean water sports of all kinds wherever it's wet, from pools to the area's many lakes and streams. Boating has always been popular. Today it's sailboats and speedboats on nearby lakes. In 1908 it was rowboats on the Blue River where the Kansas City Yacht Club had its boathouse near 15th.

parks and open spaces. Sports have a proud history and a vital presence here. In fact, spectator sports today draw more people per capita in Kansas City than in any other major league city.

A certain measure of leisure was required before sporting activities could have a chance in the hard-scrabble early life of the region. In the beginning, settlers sought out people of similar backgrounds for recreation. German and Italian neighborhoods had some of the earliest clubs and formalized social activities. By the 1870s, amateurs were organizing clubs for sport. An early gun club in 1879 became the forerunner of the Missouri State Sportsmen's Association. The first bicycle club was formed in 1882. By the 1890s the affluent were playing croquet and tennis, lining up on archery ranges and even experimenting with an odd game (introduced by several Scottish residents of Hyde Park) called *golf*.

Golf captivated a group of players who teed off on a rough course laid out in Gillham Park. After shattering a few windows in nearby residences, the players leased part of Seth Ward's cow pasture in 1896 and organized the Kansas City Country Club, which they claimed to be the first golf club in the West. The members built a clubhouse, tennis courts and a dance pavilion. When the Ward heirs sold the property in 1926 for development (the front nine was bought by Mrs. Jacob Loose to become Loose Park and the back nine went for development), the club moved to Johnson County, Kansas.

Meanwhile, golf was catching on. In 1897 the Evanston Golf Club was built near Swope Park; Independence had a country club with golf; and the Blue Hills golf course and club had been completed. Today there are 26 public courses from short and easy to very challenging, and more than 20 private courses.

Team sports also became a passion a hundred years ago. In 1893 a group of young men seeking "lawful and rational amusement" formed the Kansas City Athletic Club for handball, track and swimming. In 15 years,

the club had prospered enough to publish a magazine and sponsor carefully chosen teams of amateurs in bowling, boxing, track and basketball.

Perhaps the club's proximity to the inventor of basketball explains why its team gained national fame. After devising "roundball" in 1891, Dr. James Naismith later came to the University of Kansas, located just a few minutes away from Kansas City in Lawrence, Kansas. While he was there, Coach Naismith saw five Allen brothers from Independence play and singled out Forest Allen, later known as "Phog." As basketball fans know, the rest is American sports history.

The area's longtime link to basketball only grew stronger over the years. Into the 1940s roundball fans packed the Convention Hall to watch Amateur Athletic Union (AAU) tournaments. But college basketball soon took center court in the eyes of fans. The National Association of Intercollegiate Athletics held its first national tournament here in 1937 and it has been played here every year since, becoming one of the city's annual rites of spring.

Big Eight Conference basketball brings standing-room-only crowds to Kemper Arena, a 20,000-seat facility located in the West Bottoms near downtown. Functional and flexible, the arena was the site of both the 1976 Republican Convention and the 1985 United States Figure Skating Championships. It hosts horse shows, rodeos, dog shows, ice shows, political rallies, hockey, indoor soccer and concerts.

Like basketball, amateur football appeared in Kansas City late in the nineteenth century. Unpadded, unregulated and a bit more brutal than basketball, gridiron play caused serious bodily harm. Fatal injuries were so high — and sporting events generally so raucous — that a number of ministers tried unsuccessfully in 1897 to persuade Missouri legislators to ban football altogether.

Their efforts failed because the sport had become so popular, especially the collegiate variety. Avid fans turned the oldest football

Golf has been a favorite sport since it was introduced to the region in 1896. Today there are about 50 golf courses locally, about half of them public. Celebrity golf tournaments are important charity fundraisers. (below left) At an annual Children's Mercy Golf Classic, which benefits Children's Mercy Hospital, Lee Trevino (left in photo) and Greg Norman high-five a great putt.

Virtually every sport draws amateurs: (top) tennis players find 100 area private facilities and about 400 public courts including those at the Country Club Plaza; (left) rappellers find bluffs and outcroppings galore in this rocky landscape; and ice skaters (above) use both indoor and outdoor arenas, and sometimes frozen ponds.

"Ski Kansas City" is no joke. The Kansas City Ski Club is the nation's largest flatland ski group. The Snow Creek Ski Area in Weston, Missouri, has lighted slopes, intermediate and beginner runs served by chair lift and snow-making equipment to guarantee a full season.

rivalry west of the Mississippi, the annual meeting of the University of Missouri and the University of Kansas, into a hot contest that even today remains a special event. Amateur football at all levels is an important part of the social life of the region, and Friday nights in the fall are virtually monopolized by high school games.

The area got a professional football team in 1962 when Lamar Hunt moved his team, the Dallas Texans, to Kansas City. He re-named them the Kansas City Chiefs, in part to honor Mayor H. Roe Bartle, nicknamed "The Chief," who had encouraged the move. The team, which played a dominant role in the old American Football League, played in the first Super Bowl.

Baseball's beginnings in Kansas City were a long way from today's posh Royals Stadium, which consistently is ranked among the best parks for watching America's game. Early public games often were so rowdy and bettors so irate about the outcome that famous gunslinger Kit Carson was once hired to officiate a particularly fractious game.

In 1884 when the region's first profes-sional team, the Kansas City Unions, took the field, an afternoon at the ballpark was similar to an afternoon at a cockfight or boxing match, also popular diversions of the time. Few ladies were present, and drinking and gambling went unchecked. The Unions folded after a season; the owners tried again two years later with the Cowboys. They made it to major league status for a couple of years until 1890, when they slid to the minor leagues. There they played as the Kansas City Blues until 1955. The Blues had some good years, winning six pennants and the Little World Series in 1923.

But most notable of all the early teams was the one known as the Kansas City Mon-archs, a black ball club that barnstormed the Midwest from 1919 to 1949. The club fielded legends Satchel Paige and Jackie Robinson. Robinson eventually broke baseball's color barrier by signing with the Brooklyn Dodgers. After his success, white teams soon began

taking the best black players, and the Negro Leagues vanished.

The major league Philadelphia Athletics moved to town in 1955 and played here until the franchise shifted to Oakland, California, in 1967. They were replaced in 1969 by the Kansas City Royals, frequent contenders for the American League pennant and winners of the 1985 World Series. The Royals are so popular with Midwest fans that the team has one of the largest regional followings of any major-league franchise.

Two professional soccer teams have called Kansas City home, the Spurs and the Comets. From 1980 to 1991 the Kansas City Comets attracted fans with hard-fought games played to laser light shows, special effects and rock 'n roll music. Perhaps the team's greatest contri-bution to the area was its enthusiastic promo-tion of youth soccer, which helped make it the region's fastest growing sport for young people. Local collegiate and high school soccer teams are talented and competitive, and area players regularly find berths on regional or prestigious national teams.

If newcomers here are surprised to find vigorous soccer, rugby, field hockey, lacrosse, handball, archery, even hang-gliding — all of which flourish in parks, schools and clubs, both public and private — they are doubly amazed to discover yachting and sailing. Many lakes in the region give boaters of all interests ample places to put afloat. Even before large man-made lakes offered immense stretches of water to sail, Kansas City had its first yacht club. In 1908 the elite Kansas City Yacht Club opened on the Big Blue River with a clubhouse near where the Manchester Bridge is today.

Many sports organizations have realized that Kansas City, located on the geographical "50 yard line" or "center court" of the country, offers an ideal location for their national headquarters. Those who have found homes here include the National Collegiate Athletic Association, the National Association of Intercollegiate Athletics, the Fellowship of

Outdoor enthusiasts find almost every sport in Kansas City. (above left) The area's enormous parklands are ideal for cross-country skiing; (above) sailors and windsurfers (this one on Lake Jacomo) like winds off the prairie. The Mission Valley Hunt takes to the fields on early autumn mornings (left) and Swope Park boasts the number-one folf (frisbee golf) course (far left) of 350 nationwide. Rules of folf are similar to golf except that players throw frisbees. The 18-hole professional folf course is the home of the U.S. Open Folf Tournament held annually in June.

Worlds of Fun is a family theme park with nearly 150 rides, shows and attractions, including one of the world's tallest wooden roller coasters. Its companion park, Oceans of Fun, is a water recreation park with a million-gallon wave pool, several water slides, two lakes and various swimming pools.

Few sports go untried here. There are tracks for auto, horse and dog racing. There are lanes for bowling, with an annual spring stop of the Professional Bowlers Association Tour. Once a country club sport, tennis is now widely popular in schools as well as parks and recreation programs throughout the area. There is hunting in the fall, good fishing year round, and even competition Frisbee gets a toss.

Equestrian sports seem to go with the territory, partly because this is the home of the American Royal, the largest combined livestock, horse show and rodeo in the United States. Begun in 1899, the Royal has become a two-week-long Kansas City tradition that attracts owners and exhibitors from all over, not to mention 2,000 horses and 4,000 head of prime cattle, sheep and swine from the United States as well as Canada and other countries. Equitation riders and breeders compete before more than 300,000 spectators each year. Part of the joy of the Royal is a return to the agricultural heritage of the city with the chance to combine the shows and a stroll shoulder-to-shoulder with other sightseers through the barns and booths that accompany the events.

Kansas City has always loved to take its amusements in crowded doses. From the 1870s on, Kansas Citians found a regular opportunity for such fun in amusement parks situated on the streetcar lines. In 1907 Electric Park near Brush Creek Boulevard and The Paseo lit up entertainment possibilities. Twinkling lights illuminated fantasy scenes throughout the park, including a replica of a German village (the park was a project of Heims brewery) and an "Old Mill Stream," which carried courting couples along an artificial waterway through discreetly darkened tunnels. Fairyland Park at 79th and Prospect carried the amusement park concept even further with mechanical rides that included an enormous wooden roller coaster.

Much later, in 1972, Worlds of Fun capitalized on auto travel and outstanding technology and located a modern theme park on an interstate highway — easily accessible to traveling families in several states. Worlds of Fun was a success and was followed, in 1983, by Oceans of Fun, a huge water park. Today these are two of the area's most successful attractions.

For many who visit Kansas City, and even more for those who live here, shopping is a major attraction. Ranking seventh among the 30 largest metropolitan urban areas in per capita retail sales, with more than 340 shopping centers and myriad individual retail establishments, Kansas City is clearly a place where the tough go shopping — along with everyone else.

Shoppers of all persuasions easily find the right niche. From tony boutiques to outlet stores, the area has it all: Saks Fifth Avenue; Abercrombie & Fitch; Walton's Wholesale Club; BizMart; Sears, Roebuck and Company; the area's largest local department store operation, the Jones Store Co.; and cart vendors. In Kansas City, there is a store size and merchandising mix for just about any shopper.

Shopping districts are equally diverse. They range from the Country Club Plaza, a 14-block area known the world over as a premier shopping experience for its blend of art and lovely architecture with specialty shops, to small strip centers serving particular neighborhoods, to indoor shopping environments that provide climate control and a variety of experiences beyond simple shopping.

Crown Center, for example, offers tourists and residents an attractive mix of shops and services: dining, cinema, theater, concerts, and presentations. Weekend packages at the Westin and Hyatt Regency hotels, connected to the shops by The Link, a climate controlled walkway, draw people not only from out of state but also from the metro area itself for a mini vacation in this city-within-a-city.

Other interesting shopping destinations abound downtown, which is peppered with intriguing shops and major shopping environments such as the classy AT&T Town Pavilion. Shopping districts also can be found along such major arteries as Noland Road in

Kansas Citians love to watch and to play sports of all kinds. In addition to baseball, basketball, football and soccer (below, right), vigorous amateur softball, lacrosse, field hockey and rugby teams (above) and even polo teams (above, right) meet in parks or on organized playing fields throughout the region. Professional football is a favorite outdoor sport for thousands of fans who attend the Kansas City Chiefs games (below left) and a favorite indoor sport for thousands more who follow the team's televised play.

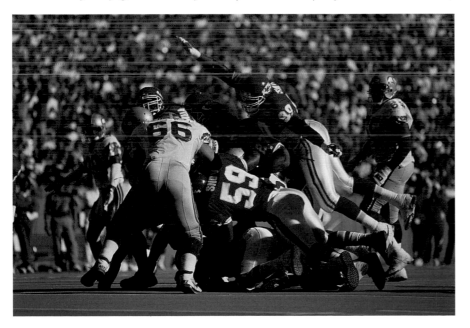

Kaleidoscope, located in Crown Center, is a children's interactive art experience that stimulates the senses and imagination with color, light, shape, texture and sound. Using materials provided by Hallmark Cards, Inc., Kaleidoscope's sponsor, young visitors turn their imaginations loose on a variety of fun art projects. A mobile version of this nationally recognized and honored children's art program hits the road in a giant trailer truck in order to bring the experience to school-age children across the country.

along such major arteries as Noland Road in Independence; the Missouri 7 corridor in Blue Springs; State Avenue in Kansas City, Kansas; the Santa Fe strip in Olathe, Kansas; the Metcalf corridor in Overland Park, Kansas; the Blue Ridge Cutoff in Grandview, Missouri; and the intersection of U.S. 69 and Missouri 10 in Excelsior Springs, Missouri.

Regional shoppers flock to huge regional malls such as Bannister Mall in eastern Jackson County and Oak Park Mall in southern Johnson County, and to smaller ones such as the Mission Center in Mission, Kansas. Colorful neighborhood areas include the Brookside Shops, Brookside Road and 63rd; Independence Square in Independence; Prairie Village at Mission Road and 71st; and the antique center at 45th and State Line Road, a mecca for antique lovers. Traditional downtown districts flourish in North Kansas City, Raytown, Belton, Lee's Summit, Liberty, Bonner Springs and Lenexa and Overland Park.

The appetite to shop appears somehow closely tied to appetite in general. Either that, or shopping is simply hungry work. As shopping opportunities have proliferated in the metro area, dining possibilities have grown apace. Once renowned as a beef and barbeque town, today Kansas City has a well-deserved reputation for culinary adventures of many kinds.

Actually, next to merchandising, "hospitality" is probably the area's oldest industry. No doubt food and drink were served to travelers by the earliest settlers, but the first written record of a dining establishment seems to be an 1846 mention of McDaniels Hostelry for Man and Beast located on the levee. Three years later, to take advantage of the '49ers headed west for gold, Dr. Benoit Troost opened what became the Gillis House on the levee between Delaware and Wyandotte. Many notable guests spent the night there during the hotel's existence, including General George Custer. Soon the little town had hospitality to spare — much of it liquid, dispensed with abandon in saloons and gaming houses that sprang up almost faster

than travelers could arrive.

Dining was as notable as drinking, with multicourse meals to fuel the appetites of drovers and gentlepersons alike. When newspaperman Charles Spalding set about to chronicle the city's development, one of the first things he observed was, "Nowhere in the states can there be found people more healthy and robust or enjoying better appetites than the people of this border."

By the 1890s, dining opportunities reflected the traditions and lifestyles of the increasingly diverse population of the region, and Kansas City became a leader in the restaurant field. The National Restaurant Association was founded here in 1919. Among other firsts to which Kansas City can lay claim are the founding of the first commercial cafeteria and the famous "Kansas City Steak," as well as the "Sizzling Steak," which usually is credited to Al Carder, who operated a restaurant in the city about 1919. Carder also is said to have invented the idea of a "menu" for restaurants, replacing the custom of serving whatever the chef felt like cooking.

But some would argue that Kansas City's greatest culinary contribution easily is barbeque. Similar in its roots to Kansas City jazz, local barbeque is a distinctive smoky, tangy creation. It had its genesis in the cooking traditions that came north during the urban migrations from Texas and the South during the 1920s. Barbeque in Kansas City is a religion and, like all matters of faith, nothing will start a quarrel faster than attempting to name the one, true "best" barbeque. Suffice it to say that more than 60 restaurants make barbeque their reason for being and that there are more variants of barbeque sauce sold here than anywhere in the country.

Native son Calvin Trillin, who has gone on to fame as a writer for *The New Yorker*, is often quoted as saying, "Not all the best restaurants in the world are in Kansas City. Only the top four or five." He may have been talking about barbeque — certainly every president of the United States who has visited

The Folly Theater (12th and Central) was built as the Standard Theater around the turn of the century. It later became a burlesque house and was slated for wrecking when citizens groups saved and restored it in 1981 as a performing arts facility. Now New Year's Eve crowds on the Barney Allis Plaza watch the top of the Folly for the lighted countdown to the New Year.

Wildwood Outdoor Education Center is a non profit educational organization that provides camp and outdoor challenge experiences in an extraordinary setting on the shores of Lake La Cygne, Kansas. Both student and adult groups take advantage of non-competitive adventure courses (left) to learn problem-solving and team-building

The American Royal Livestock, Horseshow and Rodeo, one of the nation's oldest and largest agricultural exhibitions (above), draws thousands of exhibitors and visitors each year. A traditional Kansas City social event is the presentation of the Belles of the American Royal (above right).

121

Kansas City barbeque is world-famous and the source of endless arguments: Beef or pork? Ribs or sliced meat? Which one of more than 60 barbeque establishments serves the best? Barbeque contests, especially the annual event associated with the American Royal, attract teams of amateur cooks from across the country and several Kansas City barbeque sauces are now available on supermarket shelves nationwide.

Area rodeos (right) mean excitement from barbeque to bronc bustin'.

barbeque, and Trillin is probably at the bottom of that. But it also is true that Kansas City has developed a reputation for fine food of many kinds. American, Mexican, Italian, Chinese, Greek, Japanese and what might be called Innovative Eclectic menus are the most predominant, but regional cuisines, especially Southwestern, and International, such as Thai and Indian, also have outstanding representation.

So much fun and exciting fare means visitors. One of the earliest wrote that as he stepped off a steamboat on the Kansas City Levee he felt "a stirring and vital spirit in the air." The promise of stirring experiences has built a lively visitors and convention trade in the region.

Kansas City's central location is a big plus for meeting planners — and also for vacationers. More than 55 million people are within a day's drive of Kansas City. Once here, delegates and sightseers alike are delighted by top-notch accommodations at prices lower than they expect to pay in other cities. Lodg-

ing, meals and transportation add up to a moderately priced ticket, yet the quality and diversity of Kansas City's hotels are welcome treats for visitors.

The region's convention headquarters is the Kansas City Convention Center, which covers four blocks in the heart of downtown. It includes historic Municipal Auditorium, sometimes described as one of the grandest public places in America, and H. Roe Bartle Hall, dedicated in 1976. Across the street is Barney Allis Plaza, a downtown park and public square with trees, fountains and landscaped walkways, and underneath it, parking for the Convention Center.

Other important meeting places include the John Reardon Civic Center in Kansas City, Kansas; the Kansas City Merchandise Mart and Expo Center in Overland Park, Kansas, home of the Amigo Gift Mart for wholesale buyers in the retail trade; and the Kemper Arena and American Royal Center, a 14-acre complex with three structures of indoor and outdoor exhibition and meeting space.

Most visitors agree that the best meetings of all take place face-to-face with residents who go out of their way to make strangers welcome. The local enthusiastic spirit is simply infectious. In 1975 the *Saturday Evening Post* sent writer Frederic Birmingham to Kansas City. He went away with this observation: "Kansas City, beguiling in a strangely innocent way, has invented a marvelous formula in which the stray visitor finds himself, from no matter how sophisticated a background, quietly metamorphosed into that typically Midwestern and frequently scorned creature — a booster."

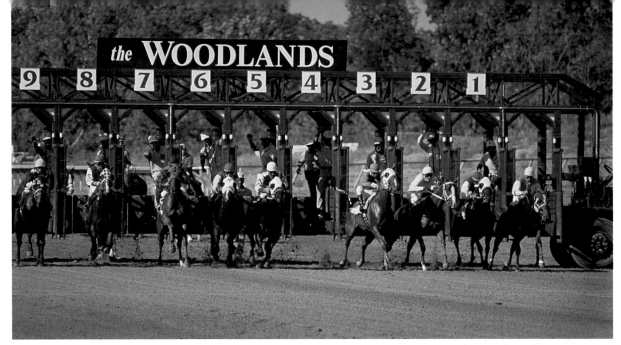

The Woodlands, a nearly $70-million track at 99th and Leavenworth Road in Kansas City, Kansas, is home to dog and horse races.

Something about the regional attitudes toward mixing work and play must build great teamwork. Area high school marching bands, drill teams and drum corps regularly win national and international honors. Drum Corp International sponsored the DCI Summer Games held in Arrowhead Stadium in 1990.

The open-air dining season is long here and restaurants throughout the metroplex offer outdoor seating.

Made world-famous by restaurant critic Calvin Trillin, Winstead's is a Kansas City institution famed for its steakburgers.

123

Kansas Citians find being outside so appealing in every season that even Santa is a little slow getting to his indoor job.

(far right) The Hospital Hill Run is Kansas City's oldest running event and annually attracts nearly 4,500 participants to try their stamina on the hilly terrain. Nationally ranked competitors join local runners for the event each year. Runners' World rates the half marathon as one of the nation's top 25.

Community

As I travel, when I come here
to the heart of the country,
my energy grows, my mind settles
and my heart smiles. For in this place,
this heart of America,
people care for one another . . .

Chief Leon Shenandoah,
Leader of the Iroquois Confederacy

A Place to Abide

The lighting ceremony on Thanksgiving evening draws as many as 250,000 people to the Country Club Plaza to cheer as 52 miles of brightly colored bulbs are switched on to light up the holiday season. The lights stay on until mid-January.

(opening) This satellite image of Kansas City by an electronic earth scanning sensor onboard the Landsat 5 satellite on October 13, 1988, was recorded by Terra-Mar Resource Information Services, Inc. Both visible and infrared images are shown, so this autumnal scene reveals heavy vegetation in bright, variegated reds and oranges. The highly reflective areas of urban development are light blue. Rivers and lakes are black.

(right) Learning activities put the whole world in the hands of sixth-, seventh- and eighth-grade students at Nowlin Middle School-Environmental Science, a Kansas City, Missouri, magnet school.

People who know Kansas City well may describe it with words like *green* and *growing*. But the complex rock formations on which this city rests also provide a vital image of the community: so many different elements brought and held together until, over time, something strong and lasting is created.

You can sense that feeling of strength and permanence when you listen to the people in this area talk, especially about what they consider uniquely "ours." Their conversation may touch upon everything from a beautiful fountain to a local company made good; the success of a sports team to the prominence of a local landmark; or maybe even a looming challenge and the way people are responding to it.

Listen more closely, and what you'll hear them really talking about is the way they feel about certain *values*, about the things they consider important. You'll hear them describing the values that make them a *community*.

Kansas City is a community made up of many cities stretching across two states and plenty of space. (There are 278 people per square mile here compared with 23,452 in New York or 2,233 in Boston.) Despite the diversity, the many geopolitical boundaries, the people of this regional metropolis are linked in an emotional partnership about what is fundamentally important in their lives — neighborhood, education, health, religion and social welfare. These are people who feel much the same way about certain values, no matter how they may differ on specific issues.

Kansas City is made up of hundreds of neighborhoods, groups of people with mutual interests or ways of looking at the world. Some are ethnic enclaves. Others are subdivisions that have attracted families with something in common, whether a love of golf or historic preservation or water sports. The metroplex offers everything from sleek penthouse apartments with river views to "rustic contemporary" suburban homes with pickled-pine country kitchens and a half-block walk to an elementary school. Neighborhoods here give residents the sense of belonging while remaining unique, a mix of shared values and individual expression.

Visitors quickly recognize similarities to their own hometowns. New Yorkers and Chicagoans are delighted by the luxury and incredible vistas offered by the towering condominiums at Crown Center or the miles of twinkling lights adorning the Country Club Plaza. San Francisco natives love the Victorian and Queen Anne homes on Union Hill or the city estates in Hyde Park. Sun-lovers from Phoenix feel at home on sunny golf course developments with contemporary link-side homes and manicured greens. Those who have lived in the nation's capital see Virginia in the comfortably elegant farm spreads (some with pastures open to the local hunt clubs) and Georgetown in the townhouses of Quality Hill, within walking distance of the businesses, theaters, shops and restaurants of downtown.

For longtime residents, their mental geography of the area is expanding to include an awareness of the world of different neighborhoods that abound here, including the ethnic neighborhoods and new suburbs of Kansas City, Kansas, and other Kansas municipalities such as Shawnee, Merriam, DeSoto and Bonner Springs; the center city's older,

When George Kessler planned the parks and boulevards system 100 years ago, he envisioned a "city within a park." Even as many smaller communities have grown together to make regional Kansas City, a park-like environment still describes the whole.

established and restored areas; the lake communities of the Northland, Lee's Summit and Blue Springs; and the suburbs ringing traditional centers in Missouri, including Independence, Raytown, Gladstone, Grandview, Claycomo, Liberty, Excelsior Springs and Richmond.

The Northland, for example, is one of the region's most scenic areas. An increasing number of people are choosing to live north of the Missouri River for its good schools, the countryside's beauty and the neighborhoods' small-town feel. They know, too, that the region's excellent highway system can put a resident of Liberty, Gladstone, Excelsior Springs or North Kansas City into a southtown job in minutes.

Meanwhile, in downtown Kansas City, an urban renaissance is under way that is making the city something of a celebrity among urban planners. What might be a volatile mix — developers, neighborhood activists and politicians — in Kansas City has become a solid partnership dedicated to returning residential stability and desirability to downtown.

For instance, the old Garment District, once one of the country's primary centers of the "rag trade," is being revived with restaurants, shops and 1,000 new housing units in what were nearly abandoned warehouses. Not far away is Union Hill, a residential development of Boston-style townhouses largely occupied by professionals and retired executives. To the south, Hyde Park and the Roanoke-Valentine area are once again thriving neighborhoods of beautifully restored larger homes, many of them late-Victorian mansions.

Neighborhood groups and homes associations have been the key to maintaining and reviving neighborhoods throughout the region. The inner city especially has found a steady strengthening through the work of citizens' coalitions. Active groups represented by the Kansas City Neighborhood Alliance are making a real difference.

Business leaders founded the Neighbor-hood Alliance in 1980 as an independent, not-for-profit corporation to serve older, low- and moderate-income areas in both Kansas City, Kansas, and Kansas City, Missouri. The purpose of the alliance is clear in its philosophy: "The most successful neighborhood programs are initiated or directed by the residents." In these areas, as is true throughout the region, neighborhoods aren't just lines on a real estate agent's map, they are places where people live together.

Across the state line in Johnson County, Kansas, young families are moving into older suburbs such as Prairie Village that were first developed soon after World War II. Farther south in Johnson County, however, is the truly burgeoning part of the metroplex. The city of Overland Park is the 26th fastest-growing city in America, and the cities of Lenexa and Olathe also are booming. Every day new residents are drawn here by schools of growing renown, new and attractive housing ranging from duplexes to elaborately planned recreational communities and ongoing, successful office and commercial developments.

To the east, in Lee's Summit, Missouri, established lake communities already provide models for the good life. Lakewood covers 2,000 acres and includes an 18-hole golf course and 300 acres of lakes. Raintree Lake offers similar amenities, and Longview Farms includes a major lake and one of the country's finest equestrian parks.

To the west in Wyandotte County, newly completed interstate highways are drawing residents and commercial development to the softly rolling landscape of eastern Kansas. Dozens of new subdivisions are developing in an area that will be one of the important growth centers of the metro region in the next 20 years.

But wherever people in this region live, one of the values they stress most is the importance of having quality education nearby for learners of all ages. The Kansas City community has a commitment to lifelong learning that offers a better future to all individuals and secures the future of the

Whatever lifestyle residents choose, Kansas City has a neighborhood to fit, including (clockwise from top) communities built around golf courses, such as Hallbrook Farms; rehabbed midtown neighborhoods, such as Longfellow; suburbs with broad lawns and nearby schools, such as Lenexa; and historic neighborhoods with restored homes, such as Pendleton Heights.

The region is served by more than 65 public libraries and several university libraries which put good books, information, programs and educational activities within the reach of every citizen. The area is also home of the Linda Hall Library of Science and Technology, the largest privately endowed scientific and technological library in the country.

community itself. This community-wide focus on improving education locally helps explain why the Kansas City area has 33 different school districts operating about 520 public schools in addition to more than 130 private and parochial schools.

The importance given to education even extends into the private sector, which is actively involved with many districts. Business is making a multimillion dollar impact on the Kansas City school system through the School/Community Partnership Program, known informally as "Adopt a School." In urban and suburban schools alike, parents and other interested adults provide support from donations of renewable resources, such as money and materials, to donations of the most precious resource, their time.

Other innovative programs capitalize on strengths in the community. Some programs are broad, such as Urban Partners, a leadership-empowerment program created by several area corporations and foundations to share business management skills with school administrators. Other initiatives are direct, such as "each-one-teach-one" volunteer tutoring in classrooms.

The success of the School/Community Partnership program is just one piece of evidence showing an urban district on the rebound. The Kansas City district offers increasingly varied curriculum choices through its magnet school program, the most ambitious in the nation. The program combines basic skills with special themed curricula designed to attract additional students to the district, to increase racial diversity and to emphasize subject excellence.

Some of the nation's finest schools can be found in Kansas City's suburbs. Schools in virtually all of the suburban districts have won recognition and various honors; the Shawnee Mission School District has been ranked among the country's top five.

For parents and pupils who desire independent education, more than 130 private and parochial schools reflecting various philoso-

phies operate within the area. A high level of cooperation exists among these schools, which have set up an association to share materials, facilities and expertise.

Another school-related organization based in Kansas City is part of the vital effort to end alcohol and drug abuse among America's teens. The National Federation of State High School Associations, creator of the guidelines for virtually every high school sport played in America, has developed a peer-based program to help student leaders in areas such as athletics, music and debate reach other students with information about chemical abuse.

Adult learners also have a world of choice in the greater Kansas City area. Degree opportunities are available at eight four-year colleges, seven junior colleges, four colleges or universities offering graduate degrees, five more colleges and universities within commuting distance, 24 business and secretarial schools, and 48 industrial and technical schools.

The area's comprehensive urban university is the University of Missouri-Kansas City, which offers undergraduate arts and science degrees and graduate degrees in the health sciences (including medicine, nursing, dentistry and pharmacy), business administration, engineering, computer science, telecommunications and performing arts.

The University of Kansas, a short commute away in Lawrence, Kansas, maintains its medical school in Kansas City, Kansas, and the Kansas Regent's Center for graduate studies in Overland Park, where metro area students can pursue both undergraduate and graduate degrees.

Publicly funded community colleges — the Metropolitan Community Colleges, Johnson County Community College and Kansas City Kansas Community College — offer two-year degree programs that support the technical needs of businesses and industries as well as provide the fundamentals for students going on to further college work. Donnelly College, a privately funded community college, provides higher education in the

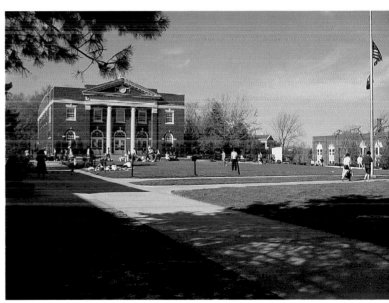

In regional Kansas City or within commuting distance are 20 institutions of higher learning. Among these are (clockwise from top left) the University of Missouri-Kansas City; Rockhurst College (Kansas City); William Jewell College (Liberty, Missouri); Longview Community College (part of Kansas City's Metropolitan Community College system); and Johnson County Community College (Overland Park, Kansas).

Research and teaching lend a deeper dimension to the quality of health care in a community. Kansas City has two medical teaching hospitals: the University of Kansas Medical Center (above), affiliated with the University of Kansas, and Truman Medical Center, the city's public hospital, affiliated with the Universiy of Missouri-Kansas City.

central city, primarily to first-generation college students.

Kansas City also has five private four-year liberal arts colleges: Avila College, Mid-America Nazarene College, Park College, Rockhurst College and William Jewell College. Among the bachelor's degree programs available at these schools are business administration, computer science, nursing, physical therapy, the humanities and natural and social sciences.

In addition to arts education to suit all interests and levels of ability, Kansas City's degree opportunities in the performing and visual arts are worthy of its status as a major cultural center. UMKC's Center for the Performing Arts is home to both undergraduate and graduate programs in music, dance and theater. The Kansas City Art Institute offers four-year degrees in the visual arts including ceramics, fiber, photography, design, painting and sculpture.

Because educational opportunities in the greater Kansas City area are outstanding — from early childhood through the most advanced training or degrees — the area boasts one of the nation's best-educated work forces.

That translates into competent employees and high productivity. It also guarantees a knowledgeable citizenry, willing and able to consider the issues that impact a community at large. Voters have consistently shown a readiness to endorse needed programs — such as a $50 million parks improvement bond issue that will renovate and expand the Kansas City Zoo.

Like education, the health of the community also is given a high priority throughout the metro area.

Residents are willing to put their money where their values are when it comes to health care. For example, a recent tax levy to provide more support for the Truman Medical Center was passed by a 2-to-1 margin. The center, which serves as the city's general hospital, is noted for offering high-quality care to area patients, including the indigent. The area also supports a number of outpatient care facilities

serving indigent and underinsured residents of the suburbs and the inner cities in both Kansas and Missouri, as well as numerous family and children's services groups.

This commitment to create a healthier community has even found expression in an effort to combat the problem of substance abuse. In a move the national media called "the country's boldest anti-drug measure," Kansas City voters also raised their sales taxes to fund a variety of programs aimed at drug-use prevention and rehabilitation.

One reason for the community's informed awareness of health issues is the impact that the medical profession has on the area. Kansas City boasts two medical schools: the University of Kansas School of Medicine at the University of Kansas Medical Center and the University of Missouri-Kansas City School of Medicine. The latter is affiliated with Truman Medical Center and is home to an innovative program in which students become physicians in six years instead of the normal eight. Both KU and UMKC have basic life sciences programs and highly regarded pharmacy schools.

Other health-related schools in the area include the University of Missouri-Kansas City Dental School; the Cleveland Chiropractic College; Research Medical Center School of Nursing; St. Luke's Hospital School of Nursing; Graceland College-Division of Nursing; The University of Kansas-College of Health Sciences; and the University of Health Sciences, an osteopathic institution. St. Luke's Hospital, Research Health Services System (formerly Research Medical Center), Menorah Medical Center and Trinity Lutheran Hospital also have residency programs in various specialities.

Schools like these have played an important role, along with private sector initiatives, in exploring new opportunities for research and discovery. One example is the Scientific Education Partnership established by the charitable foundation of Marion Merrell Dow, Inc., a global pharmaceutical company based

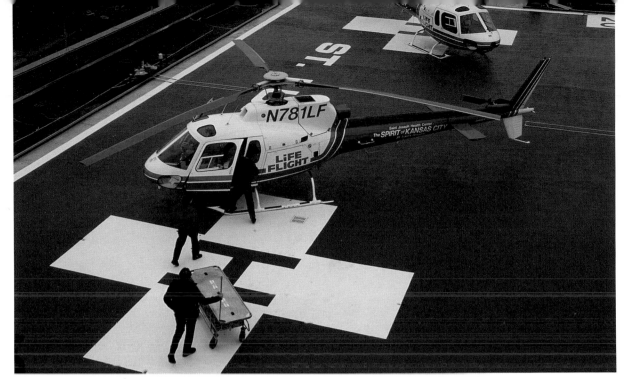

The "Spirit of Kansas City" lands on the rooftop helipad of St. Luke's Hospital, partner with St. Joseph Medical Center in operating two Life Flight "air ambulances" to transport patients within a 150-mile radius to any hospital in the Kansas City area. When St. Joseph Hospital began the helicopter service in 1977, it was only the fifth such program in the nation.

Early Kansas City health care depended heavily on the Visiting Nurses Association. Established in 1891, the organization sent nurses to the homes of the sick and operated clinics, such as a 1920 tonsils check-up (above). With a renewed emphasis on home health care, the VNA and many other visiting professionals, such as Kansas City Hospice, give welcome dimension to family health services.

(left) Established in 1861 the Kansas State School for the Deaf serves young people from pre-school to 21 years old. The Marra Museum on the school's Olathe campus is one of the few collections in the world of memorabilia and papers from the deaf community.

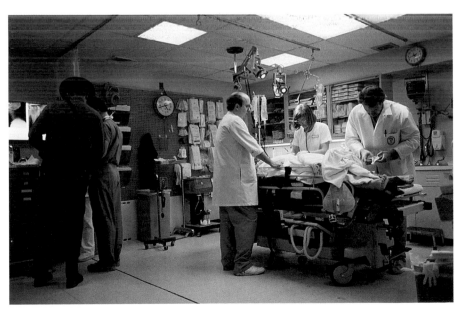

The region's outstanding health care institutions include a number of trauma centers (left) and an enormous range of specialties that serve a multistate referral area.

More than a dozen religious faiths and their variations are represented in Kansas City. As residence patterns change, congregations shift and find new buildings. The beautiful synagogue built at 3400 The Paseo for the Beth Shalom congregation is now home to a Christian congregation.

in Kansas City. The foundation put up $10 million to create a partnership with the University of Kansas and the University of Missouri-Kansas City to study diseases of the aging. The resulting intellectual center actively recruits outstanding scientists worldwide to join colleagues at both universities in biomedical studies of the aging process. Other businesses and area philanthropists have shown interest in joining this Kansas City-based research effort in the coming years.

Other important research efforts have contributed to the health sciences in Kansas City for years. Midwest Research Institute has an ongoing history of important medical research for institutional and business clients. The Linda Hall Library of Science and Technology, the largest private science library in the country, and the Cleveland Medical Library at the University of Kansas Medical Center, are known worldwide for their research holdings.

Health care also affects the region economically. Hospitals are among the area's largest employers. More than 30 of them provide quality hands-on care throughout the total spectrum of medical services. The metro region also has three freestanding rehabilitation hospitals, eight psychiatric facilities and more than a dozen skilled-nursing facilities.

As a result, Kansas City has become a regional referral center that annually attracts more than 26,000 patients from several states. They come here to receive the latest in treatments and technologies including such complex surgeries as heart, liver and kidney transplants; angioplasty; bypass surgery; lithotripsy; oncology; and sophisticated treatments for eye diseases.

Cancer treatment in Kansas City is enhanced by a number of innovative programs. The Bloch Cancer Management Center provides a 24-hour hotline for families and patients along with referrals and other assistance. A cooperative, community-wide Cancer Institute — created by Baptist Medical Center, Research Medical Center and Trinity Lutheran

Hospital — combines the experience of their oncology teams and shares state-of-the-art equipment to permit more cost-effective treatment for patients. The University of Kansas Medical Center is involved in significant cancer research and offers important research-and-screening programs to the public. St. Luke's Hospital Cancer Center emphasizes research and clinical treatment.

In the last few years, hospitals and other health care providers throughout the community have redesigned their systems to meet many new challenges. One example is Kansas City Hospice, one of the nation's pioneering hospice groups. What began as a small grassroots effort only a few years ago, today provides humane assistance to hundreds of terminally ill patients and their families.

In such times of crisis, as well as in times of thanksgiving, most area residents find strength in deeply held beliefs. For some, these are simply standards of responsible behavior. For most, however, they are standards of faith. And the spiritual well-being of the metro region is the concern of more than a dozen religions.

The faith of the people here is richly diverse and complex. In 1988 representatives of the world's faiths met in Wichita, Kansas, for what some theologians called the most important meeting of its kind since the World's Parliament of Religions in 1893. Of all the cities represented, Kansas City sent the largest, most varied delegation.

But what else might be expected of an area settled by so many different peoples under such difficult conditions? As one pioneer wrote in his diary about the vast nights at the edge of the prairie: "It's easy to think about God out here. You'd be a fool not to."

Area worshippers are most likely to belong to one of the region's dominant faiths: Protestant, Catholic, Jewish, Eastern Orthodox or Islamic. But there are also worshipers who are Hindu, Buddhist, Sufi, Baha'i, Native American, Sikh, Jain, Zoroastrian or Unitarian Universalist. They meet in churches, cathe-

Dedicated in 1988, the Jewish Community Campus at 5811 West 115th in Overland Park reflects a migration of Jewish families to south suburban neighborhoods. The major Jewish organizations are housed in the 224,000 square-foot facility.

The landmark Cathedral of the Immaculate Conception (411 West 11th) is a reminder amid the halls of commerce of the life of the spirit. Built in 1882, the cathedral has a 23-karat gold leaf dome that is a distinctive feature of the Kansas City skyline.

Special traditions in many congregations are shared with the community at large, especially at holidays. Here the Kansas City Baptist Temple (5460 Blue Ridge Cut-Off) creates a "living Christmas tree."

The Shrine of Our Lady of Guadalupe on West 23rd has been a spiritual center for the West Side community and Hispanic people of Kansas City. Bought from its former Lutheran membership, it was dedicated as a Catholic church in 1922. Today the church is used for special occasions and celebrations. Nearby is the Guadalupe Center Inc., a community-based organization that provides social services to the Hispanic community.

Competing in sports through Special Olympics programs is one of several activities available to people with disabilities. Reflecting the sturdy will-to-prevail that characterizes so many people throughout the metroplex, support services abound for people with disabilities or illnesses and for their families. In addition to rehabilitation and healing, these groups, along with organizations such as The Whole Person Inc., seek independence and productivity for people with disabilities. They have made important progress toward the goal of making Kansas City truly accessible to all.

drals, synagogues, storefronts, gymnasiums, private homes, tents, stadiums and arenas. Congregations range from intimate prayer circles to services for thousands.

Several denominations have their world headquarters in the area: The Church of the Nazarene in Kansas City; The Reorganized Church of Jesus Christ of the Latter Day Saints in Independence; and Unity School of Christianity near Lee's Summit. These also are three of the world's major religious publishers: Herald House, the publishing arm of the RLDS; Nazarene Publishing House; and the publishing arm of Unity.

Four seminaries are here: Saint Paul School of Theology, a United Methodist seminary, (which counts among its graduates Kansas City's first black mayor, the Reverend Emanuel Cleaver); Midwestern Baptist Theological Seminary; Central Baptist Theological Seminary; and Nazarene Theological Seminary.

Among the religious-affiliated colleges in the area are Rockhurst College, one of 28 Jesuit colleges in the United States; Avila College, a Catholic four-year college; Donnelly College, the only Catholic diocesan junior college in the country with a specific commitment to the inner city; Park College, in Parkville, Missouri, which is owned by the RLDS; and William Jewell, with a Baptist affiliation.

Religious celebration in the community extends to interfaith groups, observances and festivals. Interfaith cooperation and ecumenical activities have been important to Kansas City's religious life since the beginning. The first recorded exchange of pulpits was in 1890 when Episcopal Bishop B.B. Ussher of Christ Church spoke at B'nai Jehudah and Rabbi Henry Berkowitz returned the visit. On St. Patrick's Day in 1895, Rabbi Samuel Schulman was the principal speaker at a gathering in Kansas City of 3,000 Irish-American Catholics. His theme was a philosophy that has permeated the religious life of Kansas City for a hundred years: "reverence for the sacredness of conscience."

Present-day interfaith observances include the Martin Luther King Jr. Birthday Celebration (now a major community event) and the National Day of Prayer. Ministerial associations hold annual interfaith Thanksgiving services, and groups such as the United Prayer Movement welcome all faiths.

Since 1987 more than 25 religious leaders have met for discussions as part of the Christian-Jewish-Muslim Dialogue Group. The Kansas City Interfaith Council, composed of representatives from 12 faiths, works to educate the Kansas City community about the similarities and differences in religious beliefs shared throughout the area.

For many, an important dimension of the inspired life is the call to care for others. In Kansas City, early benevolence was a function of ethnic connection or religious belief. Immigrants turned to each other for mutual aid by forming benevolence societies. The Irish had their Hibernian Society; the Germans their Turnverein; the Poles, the Polish National Alliance; the Greeks, the Annunciation Community.

Without a doubt, the efforts of the Jewish community to help its own were among the most extensive and innovative of all the immigrant groups. Early Jewish settlers were, for the most part, German Reform Jews whose education and skills helped them integrate quickly and prosperously into the area. Their efforts set in place a model for the social welfare infrastructure of the greater Kansas City community.

In 1901 the United Jewish Charities was formed to consolidate assistance efforts. And Jewish social activists did not always limit their work to Jews. As early as 1884 Rabbi Joseph Krauskopf formed the nonsectarian "Poor Man's Free Labor Bureau" to help find work for the poor of all creeds.

All organized religious groups offered aid and comfort to their congregants, but another that built a number of lasting charitable institutions was the Roman Catholic Church. In the beginning, it was largely represented in this area by Irish settlers. The Catholic Family

Camp Opportunity (below left) provides camping experiences for children with special needs. Harvesters-The Community Food Network (above) is a community wide effort to feed the hungry through volunteer efforts and donations from individuals, businesses (including restaurants and other food services) and foundations. The United Way Pre-school (right) helps meet the childcare needs of low-income families.

Getting together is an important aspect of the social service network in the area. Here, visiting middle school students join the seniors who meet each week to play bingo at Casa Feliz (2600 Belleview), a senior citizens' center and nutrition site on Kansas City's West Side.

Kansas City is proud to be designated a Clean Air City, and many neighborhoods have initiated successful residential recycling. Citizens of all ages throughout the region are working on environmental issues. One event on Earth Day 1991 featured a "Styrosauras Rex" from styrofoam containers.

and Children's Services carries on a tradition of caring begun when Kansas City's first priest, Father Bernard Donnelly, organized assistance programs for arriving Catholics.

Today civic and charitable efforts increasingly are non-sectarian. The secular roots of organized charity, however, can be traced back to such groups as the Women's Christian Temperance Union. It was organized here in 1870 to provide shelter, jobs and general assistance. Their work concentrated more and more on women and children; in 1883, they founded the Gillis Orphans' Home.

To cope with the ills created by the unsettled economy of the 1880s and 1890s, the Kansas City Provident Association (today it is known as Family & Children's Services) was formed in 1880, followed by the Helping Hand Institute in 1894. By the turn of the century, social settlement houses were numerous and efforts to get the poor into employment of some kind dominated charitable endeavor. "Workhouses" and "industrial institutes" were set up to teach domestic and factory skills.

But even in charity, Kansas Citians aspired to do the job well and efficiently. Philanthropist William Volker spurred the formation in 1908 of the city's — and the nation's — first Board of Public Welfare. Volker wanted to apply business principles to benevolence. Private charities already had formed the Associated Charities in 1899 to coordinate their efforts. By the end of World War I, charitable endeavor was even better organized. In 1920, 54 local charities participated with the Chamber of Commerce in a funding campaign and the annual Charities' Campaign (now the United Way) was begun.

The barn-raising spirit that turns out to help a neighbor grew ever more deeply rooted in the regional psyche. In the next few decades, charities expanded their role, from neighborhood and church groups to the establishment of such major charitable trust funds as the William T. Kemper Foundation, the Ewing Kauffman Foundation and the Hall

Family Foundations which, as one of the city's largest and most influential charitable entities, concentrates today on such areas of local emphasis as support of major visual and performing arts institutions, economic development of the central city and civic and community issues of high priority.

In all such efforts, Kansas City showed itself to be a caring community. It has always been blessed with more than its share of volunteers — more than the national average of one in two adults — and major philanthropic benefactors. Business and professional people annually team up to winterize inner-city homes. A rare spirit of cooperation among social service agencies and not-for-profit organizations has created unique programs for the elderly, the very young and the very poor, including an area-wide homelessness prevention effort that serves as a national model for other cities. One part of this is Open Hearts/Open Homes, a program that places homeless families with volunteer host families.

The Kansas City Dream Factory, which fulfills the dreams of terminally and chronically ill children, has granted more than half of all the wishes fulfilled by the 26 Dream Factory chapters nationwide.

Large scale philanthropy in the area received a boost when the Kansas City Association of Trusts and Foundations was formed in 1949 and again, in 1976 when the Clearinghouse for Mid-Continent Foundations was established to bring together grantors and grantees. In 1979 The Greater Kansas City Community Foundation and Affiliated Trusts was created, representing a broad base of donors and programs. Today it is one of the largest and most active community foundations in the nation, involved in a broad range of efforts to address issues affecting the quality of life in the community.

Quality of life means different things to different individuals. For a community to achieve greatness, the chances to pursue quality — however a person defines it — must be equal for all. Increasingly Kansas City has

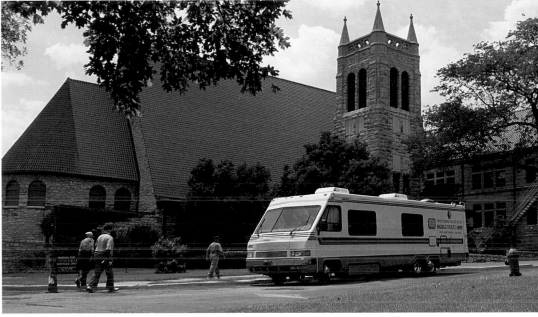

To get health care to homeless people, the Swope Parkway Health Center fields a rolling clinic, medically equipped and staffed. The van visits more than 20 sites throughout the metropolitan area providing medical and social services. The team stops in places where the homeless can be found from empty buildings to established homeless outreach programs, such as the one at Grace and Holy Trinity Cathedral (above, at 13th and Broadway). Swope Parkway Medical Center is the area's major provider of medical and mental health services to the medically indigent and is recognized nationally as one of the country's outstanding community health centers.

The innovative Shepherds Centers of America began in Kansas City. The Shepherd Center is a program in which senior citizens help each other maintain independent and productive lifestyles through activities ranging from meal delivery (above) to legal counseling. At least once a week, members gather (top) for fellowship, classes and discussion groups. Today the concept has created more than a hundred centers nationwide, with new sites opening every year.

Area police departments offer educational and community programs to share safety information and to interact regularly with citizens. The message: keeping down crime is everyone's job. Here the "heat" takes a break as a Kansas City, Missouri, policeman combats summer.

come to value the differences between ethnic and cultural groups, differences that broaden possibilities and enrich community life.

Harmony in a World of Difference is an innovative project designed to increase understanding of different groups and reduce prejudice in homes, schools, workplaces, houses of worship — and hearts. Supported by businesses, not-for-profit agencies, foundations and private donors, Harmony seeks to improve race relations and increase cultural awareness.

Through the program, multicultural aids and a Harmony curriculum are made available to schools. Media supporters have provided many hours of programming. Harmony Alliance, a network of organizations and individuals intent on building relationships across racial, cultural, and religious barriers, sponsors events to encourage cross-cultural understanding.

Perhaps more than any other single effort, Harmony speaks to the future of community in Kansas City. Our strength and the identity of our city is in our differences, combined by mutual respect into a sense of community, into something strong and lasting.

Ethnic festivals punctuate the calendar. (above) Chinese New Year is ushered in by the traditional dragon, and (right) the Italian community, especially in the Northeast neighborhoods, is always glad for a reason to celebrate. The dances of Mexico, performed by several local troupes, are favorites at city-wide festivals (far right).

The Kansas City Highland Games and Scottish Festival annually offers highland dancing, piping and drumming and bagpipe band competitions.

Children on a float in the St. Patrick's Day parade display costumes of various ethnic groups in the region.

Kansas City welcomes strangers with a hospitality many visitors find amazing. Consequently, people come back again and again. The streets of downtown Kansas City become a sea of blue jackets when the Future Farmers of America come to town every fall as they have for more than 60 years.

Thousands of Boy Scouts and their parents, leaders and friends pledge allegiance to the flag at a Heart of America Scouting Expo in Swope Park in 1990.

Companionship takes many forms: (left) a Kansas City, Missouri, firefighter and friend; (above) a children's fun run in Mill Creek Park; (below) warming the bench.

Maxey Dupree (right) was a legendary figure of friendliness in Kansas City. For 12 years, from his position as a crossing guard at 33rd and Southwest Trafficway, he daily warmed the hearts of morning work-bound drivers with his joyful waves. In his memory, the Stop Violence Coalition and a local television station established the Maxey Dupree Humanitarian Award, given annually to three adults who exemplify kindness and goodwill. The nominees are selected through essays written by children from 60 area schools.

(right) Near the airport is the Heart Forest, an arboreal celebration of the heartland. The heart-shaped forest was designed by "land painter" Stan Herd, and funded and planted by individuals and companies from all over the region. Coordinated by the Heart Peace Institute, which annually sponsors the World Peace Celebration on New Year's Eve, the forest was initially created as an impetus to Kansas Citians to think globally. As the trees grow, it will become an increasingly visible emblem of Kansas City's commitment to global and environmental issues — and a striking welcome to air travelers arriving in the heart of America.

144

Epilogue

The trip from one state to another is a daily occurrence for many area residents including these children crossing State Line Road in their neighborhood.

In the late twentieth century in America, Kansas City is a city moving into its own, still facing the best years ahead. Not years of out-of-control growth or boom-and-bust development, but years of steadiness and strength, the kind of years anyone would want for the next generations.

From the beginning, that is all anyone has ever asked of Kansas City: the chance to work hard and to succeed in a place where they, their children and their children's children can live happily.

Time and again, newcomers say they've come here because it seemed like a good place for children. Or longtime residents say they stayed for the same reason. They generally list good schools, parks, art, sidewalks, friendly people, neighborhoods where children can ride a bike or play ball in the street after dinner. They talk about small town values and big city opportunities. A few try to describe a certain spirit, a kind of promise they feel here.

Kansas City simply feels like a place where life will still be worth living generations from now. It may just be the ideal American city for the twenty-first century; manageable in size but generous in land area, centrally located, economically resilient. More important, it is populated by a fundamentally decent people at a time when decency increasingly will be a precious resource, perhaps the planet's only salvation.

If forecasters are right, the twenty-first century will usher in a period of restoring nature's harmonies and rediscovering human values. It will be a time when agriculture and information will be crucial to keeping the people

of the global village fed and functioning in an increasingly complex world. These predictions describe a role in the drama of history for which Kansas City has long rehearsed.

From its raw beginnings, Kansas City has long straddled the fence between becoming civilized and "lighting out for the territories," as fictional Missourian Huck Finn did. Huck's point of view about getting *too* civilized was absolutely Midwestern. In Kansas City, things were always up to date: industry flourished, business thrived, government modernized. But something about the place resisted the pell-mell pace of life (and the sometimes unfortunate consequences) of the urban fast track.

Always a little too willing to compare itself to other places, always a little fearful of being out of sync with the times, Kansas City began to fret that it wasn't better known. In the 1970s, a small group of business leaders created Prime Time, a program to tell the national and international media that Kansas City was in its prime and was not a cowtown in any way, shape or form. They called on opinion-makers on the coasts and some spots in between. They invited the media to town. The city shone.

In 1976, Prime Time paid off, and the Republicans held their national convention in Kansas City. The media wrote delighted-to-be-so-surprised reports from what they came to call "the last livable city." One BBC correspondent proclaimed, "If Kansas City were in Europe, everyone would rave about it."

During this effort, the president of Midwest Research Institute, Dr. Charles N. Kimball, himself a transplanted Boston native, talked about his adopted town in farsighted terms that now have the ring of gospel.

"There are two persistent fallacies about

urban America: that bigness brings greatness and that continued growth is a fatalistic reality beyond our control. Size, once a positive attribute of cities, has become an albatross around their necks . . . controlled growth may be the only answer. Cities of manageable size, like Kansas City, are more sensible, less costly, less damaging to the countryside and more rewarding in human values."

Kansas City is becoming the city others use as a standard of comparison. The news has gotten out that this is a place to make a life of quality.

No one has to be worried any longer that this is a cowtown. Not when cowtown is synonymous with hicktown, anyway. But a frontier town? That's something else. Maybe it's time to quit resisting Western imagery and admit that this is certainly a city with a frontier attitude.

Frontier doesn't mean board sidewalks, as anyone who's been to Kansas City knows. It does mean a stirring, energetic place where people of vision and hope may meet on their paths to a better life.

Whether they took wagons west or settled here to build a future for themselves and their families, travelers once knew this spot as a starting place on the trail of dreams.

It still is, even now, when our frontiers may be beyond the stars. More than ever, our journeys need a starting point so much at the heart of what is important that it remains a sustaining image of what is possible and valuable, and what is worth returning to, again and again.

Even when humankind's frontiers are beyond the moon and stars, Kansas City will still be a fine place for beginning — and ending — a journey.

Acknowledgments

The creation of *Kansas City* (like the development of the city itself) is the story of many people joining together their skills and interests to build something far greater than their separate abilities would allow. We would like to thank them for their contributions.

In large part, this book exists because of the outstanding work of Jane Mobley, Vivian Strand and Michael DeMent, who made up the primary project team.

Michael DeMent served as project manager for *Kansas City*, holding together the many disparate elements of its preparation. His skills as a writer and editor are evident throughout the book. Less obvious, but perhaps more important, is the coordination of so many people's efforts — everyone who worked on photographs, copy, editing, production, printing and binding — into a wonderful whole with all involved still enthusiastic about working together and about the book.

Jane Mobley is a talented and experienced writer who brought great insight and determination to this project. One of the more difficult aspects of a book like *Kansas City* is finding the interesting anecdote, the little-known fact. Jane's affection for this city is easy to see in the stories she's found which provide much of the richness of *Kansas City* . Vivian Strand is a gifted designer who combines a keen eye, great patience and a commitment to making design serve the subject at hand. Her skills are reflected in work that allows the city to speak for itself without interference or artifice. Separately, Jane and Vivian are exceptional individuals; together, they are a remarkable team.

Producing this book involved the daunting challenge of matching the standard of quality established by the first two editions of *Kansas City*. The guiding force behind those earlier volumes was Bill Johnson, who recognized 20 years ago that Kansas City deserved a book of its own. He generously shared his wisdom and experience on this edition. His suggestions were greatly appreciated.

The project team is especially indebted to Sue Morey for her help in pulling together so much of the photography for Kansas City. She maintained the team's peace of mind through her good humor, her ability to communicate the book's needs to photographers and her steadfast and capable administration of the images they created.

Special thanks also go to Galt Piper for helping ensure that Hallmark photographers were on hand to document many special moments in the community's day-to-day life. Work for this book was not an assignment, but a labor of love as Hallmark photographers participated on their own time.

The historical elements of this project came from archives, historical societies, museums, libraries and private collections throughout greater Kansas City. For the most part, we have tried to find photos rarely seen by the public. Much of the collection required was performed by Andrea Whitmore. Her dedication, judgment, and delight in the material were important to the finished book.

We are very thankful to the professional and volunteer staffs of all the organizations in the area with special interests in regional history, particularly the Kansas City Museum, the Western Historical Manuscripts Collection, the Missouri Valley Room of the Kansas City Public Library, the Jackson County Historical Society, the Raytown Historical Society, the Kansas Room of the Johnson County Library, and the Board of Parks and Recreation of Kansas City, Missouri.

In addition, many corporations, professional organizations, businesses, associations, and institutions shared materials with us. We are especially grateful for their help.

A number of people helped move the book along from day to day. Charlie Hucker and Andy McMillen provided incisive input on all elements of the project. Beth Scalet made important improvements through her copyediting and proofreading. Licia Clifton-James' administrative support kept the myriad changes in copy smooth and orderly. We likewise appreciate the copyediting work of Sheila Strand; proofreading support given by Peggy Skerko, Gillian Findlay, Debbie Seely and Lyn Foister; the historical research of Nancy Harris; organization of materials and fact-checking by Colette Panchot; administrative help from Molly Maxwell and Sarah Hofstra; and contractual support by Carol Gibson and Sharon Schreiber. We are thankful to them all.

A project of this nature is affected by many individuals whose contributions are influential but generally unremarked. The beautiful calligraphy was penned by Jan Powell. Behind the scenes support was provided by Phillip Hofstra, Mark Kolar and Linda Collier who listened patiently to ideas, problems and too much Kansas City trivia.

And finally, those of us who worked on this book are unabashed fans of this city. We appreciate the opportunity given to us by Don Hall, chairman of Hallmark Cards, to share our enthusiasm for Kansas City with others.

Photo Credits

American Heartland Theater: *105, inside theater.* **Todd Balfour**: *34, Moore sculpture.* **Alison K. Barnes**: *2, wheat.* **The Arch Diocese of Kansas City-St. Joseph/"The Catholic Key"**: *137, Shrine of Our Lady of Guadalupe.* **Bob Barrett**: *12, Rozzelle Court; 12, St. Patrick's Day Parade; 23, Clark Point; 30, Mineral Hall; 31, Weatherby Lake; 32, Oppenstein Memorial Park; 33, Shoal Creek; 38, Fort Osage; 41, Huron Cemetery; 51, Wornall Home; 94, Women's Jazz Festival; 95, "I Love KC Art"; 97, Kansas City Museum; 98, Count Basie; 99, Musicians Mutual building; 103, Mariachi band; 116, Snow Creek; 121, American Royal; 123, Winstead's restaurant; 142, Chinese New Year; 142, Italian Festival.* **Talis Bergmanis**: *vi, Scout; 7, stockyards; 25, daffodils; 25, hot air balloons; 29, flamingos; 32, Plaza tile; 32, tile on porch; 33, Liberty Memorial frieze; 34, ice on river; 34, woman in snow; 35, flash cube building; 70, cement worker; 75, Wolf Creek power plant; 75, KCPL power plant; 80, KCPL building; 117, cross-country skiing; 125, race; 130, aerial of neighborhood; 131, Longfellow neighborhood; 143, FFA crowd.* **Children's Mercy Hospital**: *9, Tom Watson.* **Convention and Visitors Bureau of Greater Kansas City**: *65, Rosedale Arch.* **Copaken White & Blitt**: *85, Renaissance buildings.* **Kevin Cozad**: *122, rodeo rider; 143, Scottish Highlands festival.* **Crittenton/Clayton O'Connor**: *9, PGA Senior Classic.* **Crown Center Redevelopment Corporation/James Maidhof**: *10, wheelchair racers.* **Dinner Playhouse, Inc.**: *106, dinner theater performer.* **David Dumay**: *1, Kansas City skyline; 3, Chiefs crowd; 7, firemen; 10, downtown basketball; 11, American Royal Parade; 11, blues man; 15, Hotel guests; 15, high school football; 16, Habitat for Humanity; 39, Pioneer Mother; 71, downtown traffic; 91, downtown buildings; 110-111, Royals stadium; 143, children on float.* **John Eagan**: *8, RLDS Auditorium; 9, Children's Mercy Hospital; 17, Truman Home; 101, mural for RLDS Temple; 102, Benton mural; 128, Plaza lights; 131, Hallbrook; 137, Living Tree; 139, Camp Opportunity; 143, Boy Scouts.* **Anne Echeberria**: *100, Plaza Art Fair.* **Federal Reserve Bank of Kansas City**: *82, bank lobby.* **Steven Ginn**: *13, Native Americans in group; 25, fall in park; 27, Brush Creek; 107, War dancer; 119, rugby; 119, amateur soccer.* **Jeri Gleiter**: *4, Kansas River; 4, Missouri Queen; 5, Quality Hill; 5, balloons over suburbs; 18, tree aerial; 18, sunset on trees; 24, farmland aerial; 49, Civil War reenactment; 57, Union Cemetery; 72, grain elevators; 73, Yellow Freight; 73, burning field; 77, railroad yard aerial; 83, Kansas City, Kansas; 124, boy fishing.* **Richard Gunn**: *112, polo player; 115, Plaza tennis; 117, hunt with dogs.* **Hallmark Cards, Inc.**: *viii, "Kansas City Spirit," Norman Rockwell; 16, 1951 flood.* **Doug Hamer**: *30, shirtwaist house; 83, Reardon Convention Center; 83, Bartle Hall; 86, Linwood Shopping Center; 99, Kansas City Symphony; 101, man at art fair; 103, man with guitar in park; 108, State Ballet of Missouri; 109, Starlight Theater; 121, Folly Theater; 124, Santa Claus; 123, drum and bugle corp.* **Heart Peace Institute/Jon Blumb**: *145, aerial view of Heart Forest.* **Kevin Hosley**: *15, downtown buildings; 73, tractor; 81, Fairfax GM plant; 90, U.S. Sprint; 137, cathedral.* **Howard Needles Tammen & Bergendoff**:

85, Missouri Public Service building. **Roy Inman**: *4, Muse fountain; 8, Greek Orthodox church; 27, Verona Columns; 27, columns on Gregory Boulevard; 27, Freedom Fountain; 29, Mill Creek Park fountain; 31, Olathe home; 41, Grinter house; 55, Mahaffie Farm; 59, Longview Farm; 63, 1959 car show; 65, Trail of Treaties March; 66, 1960s shopping; 68-69, Metcalf at College Boulevard with lightning; 73, North Kansas City shopping district; 75, oil derrick; 76, barge on river; 77, Kansas City International Airport; 79, Poinsettia greenhouse; 81, Green Mill Candy; 82, Federal Building; 84, River Market; 85, Corporate Woods; 87, auction school; 87, Brookside shopping district; 96, Nelson painting; 101, Lenexa 3D Art Fair; 101, Christo walkways; 103, Missouri Town; 104, Kansas City Youth Symphony; 115, golfers at Cedar Creek; 117, frisbee golf; 120, Kaleidoscope; 123, outdoor restaurant; 124, hang glider; 131, Lenexa; 131, Pendleton Heights; 135, Kansas School for the Deaf; 137, Jewish Community Center.* **Jackson County Historical Society**: *17, Shubert Theater; 51, J.C. Hall's first office; 53, garment district; 61, WPA; 66, 1955 skyline; 81, 1951 car plant.* **J. C. Nichols Company**: *56, J. C. Nichols hiking; 56, Verona Columns.* **Johnson County Community College**: *105, Cultural Education Center.* **Kansas City Art Institute/Frankie Messer**: *97, sculptures.* **Kansas City Friends of Alvin Ailey**: *108, dance group.* **The Kansas City Jewish Chronicle/Kevin Blayney**: *136, former Beth Shalom.* **Kansas City Board of Parks & Recreation**: *26, West Bluffs; 62, Plaza in the 1940s; 75, Penn Valley Park; 114, Kansas City Yacht Club.* **Kansas City, Missouri, Public Library; Missouri Valley Special Collections**: *5, Cully Town; 6, Wiedenmann store; 6, Tivoli gardens; 40, Levee; 40, Kanzas City; 41, Hannibal bridge; 42, Main Street; 43, City Market 1878; 43, City Market 1893; 43, City Market 1940s; 45, Wide Awake; 45, 9th Street Incline; 48, 22nd & Wyandotte; 49, 6th and Minnesota; 50, Fire Team; 51, Teddy Roosevelt parade; 51, General Hospital; 53, auto show; 55, Union Station 1920; 55, Armistice Day 1919; 56, Signboard Hill; 58, women aviatrixes; 61, cattle show; 61, stoplight on Linwood; 74, Coates House; 79, Board of Trade 1925.* **Kansas City, Missouri Public Schools**: *129, Nowlin school.* **Kansas City Museum**: *14, 1903 flood; 36-37, Petticoat Lane; 41, steamboats; 44, early cable car; 45, electric cable car; 47, Loula Long; 49, William R. Nelson; 49, Robert T. Van Horn; 49, Louis Hammerslough; 52, car and cycle group; 54, 12th and Walnut; 55, Pisciotti delivery; 60, Pla Mor 1933.* **Kansas City Southern Industries/Tal Wilson**: *77, railroad yard.* **Fred Kautt**: *113, Crown Center Concert; 119, polo players; 119, Chiefs football game.* **David Lopez**: *13, Hispanic Festival; 99, jazz club; 142, Mexican dancers.* **Lyric Opera**: *105, opera performance.* **Martin City Melodrama/R. H. Rusty Wooldridge**: *104, melodrama performance.* **Bruce Mathews**: *22, Northland Fountain; 31, Union Hill Arts; 47, Shawnee Indian Mission; 53, Alexander Majors House; 79, Board of Trade; 87, Independence Center; 87, Town Pavilion; 88, NCAA building; 89, underground caves; 123, Woodlands; 132, Lucille Bluford Library; 144, Maxey Dupree; 144, Mill Creek Park fun run.* **Ninette Maumus**: *14, veterans with flag; 16, whittling hands; 17, World*

Series parade; 117, windsurfing. **Mark McDonald**: *33, the Link walkway; 67, 1985 skyline; 78, man on girders; 85, PARS buildings; 121, Botar Ball; 133, Longview College; 139, United Way pre-school; 141, Swope Parkway Health Center van.* **Midwest Research Institute**: *63, 1950s lab.* **Michael A. Mihalevich**: *28, the "Thinker"; 66, 1976 Republican Convention; 84, City Market; 88, Kemper Arena; 92-93, Nelson-Atkins Museum; 103, Renaissance Festival; 115, boys rappelling; 140, styrosaurus; 144, fireman and friend; 147, moon over skyline.* **Missouri Repertory Theatre**: *105, performance.* **John Perryman**: *7, Stephenson's Apple Orchard; 11, sandlot baseball; 19, fireworks; 64, Liberty Memorial; 83, Barney Allis Plaza; 89, El Tacquito; 89, Boulevard Beer; 97, Toy and Miniature Museum; 107, tap dance class; 139, Harvesters; 141, Shepherds Center; 141, Meals on Wheels.* **National Agricultural Center and Hall of Fame**: *61, farm implements.* **The Negro League's Baseball Museum**: *63, Monarchs.* **Raytown Historical Society**: *53, Raytown drug store.* **Sealright, Midwest Division/Ron Berg, Vedros & Associates**: *90, man with labels.* **Phil Smith**: *18, sunset over water; 25, Squaw Creek.* **Special Olympics of Kansas**: *130, race.* **St. Luke's Hospital**: *135, Life Flight; 135, emergency room.* **St. Joseph Medical Center**: *47, radiology room.* **Vivian Strand**: *124, bicycle riders; 139, bingo.* **Terra-Mar Resource Information Services, Inc., Mountain View, California**: *126-127, Landsat Satellite Image.* **Unity Village**: *89, tower at Unity Village.* **University of Kansas Medical Center/Shari Hartbauer**: *134, doctors in training.* **University of Missouri-Kansas City**: *133, music students.* **Carol Vanderwal**: *20-21, Loose Park rose garden.* **Visiting Nurses Association**: *135, children's checkup.* **Watkins Mill/Cindy Brown**: *43, outside view of mill.* **Walt Whitaker**: *11, barbeque; 29, Burr Oaks Nature Center; 65, Vietnam Veterans Memorial; 72, trolley; 97, Strawberry Hill Museum; 122, barbeque contest; 133, Rockhurst College; 133, William Jewell College; 133, Johnson County Community College classroom.* **Wildwood Outdoor Education Center**: *121, adventure course.* **Steve Wilson**: *106, Nutcracker ballet; 108, City in Motion; 115, Crown Center ice skaters.* **Worlds of Fun/Oceans of Fun**: *17, swimmers in tubes; 118, roller coaster.* **Young Company, Inc./Hank Young**: *13, the Marching Cobras; 29, Monarch butterflies; 34, foggy lane; 46, child by tent; 79, Weston tobacco fields; 81, ARMCO steel; 90, fiber optics; 107, dancer from India; 115, Greg Norman; 141, policeman; 144, boys blowing bubbles; 146, children crossing State Line Road.* **John Zaiger**: *45, Jesse James house.*

Kansas City
A Celebration of the Heartland

was digitally composed in Minion and Palatino
and printed on Warren's Lustro Offset Enamel Dull,
a neutral pH paper with an expected 300-year
library-storage life as determined by the
Council of Library Resources of the
American Library Association.